BORDER PATROL

Perkins in 1918 in the Immigration Service.

Border Patrol

With the U.S. Immigration Service
On the Mexican Boundary 1910-54

by

CLIFFORD ALAN PERKINS

Assisted by
NANCY DICKEY

Edited with an Introduction by
C. L. SONNICHSEN

C. L. Sonnichsen (signature)

TEXAS WESTERN PRESS
THE UNIVERSITY OF TEXAS AT EL PASO
1978

COPYRIGHT 1978

TEXAS WESTERN PRESS

THE UNIVERSITY OF TEXAS AT EL PASO

•

Photographs by

W. D. SMITHERS

•

Design by

EVAN HAYWOOD ANTONE

Library of Congress Catalog Card Number 77-91576

ISBN 0-87404-058-2

CHAPTERS

Introduction vii

TUCSON

I	*Getting Started*	1
II	*The Chinese Invasion*	7
III	*On Duty*	15

EL PASO

IV	*On the Fringes of Revolution*	32
V	*The Daily Grind*	44
VI	*Border Problems*	54
VII	*Death in Uniform*	65
VIII	*Up the Ladder*	72
IX	*Prohibition*	83
X	*Border Patrol*	89

SAN ANTONIO

IX	*Down the Rio Grande*	100
XII	*Problems and Solutions*	109

TIJUANA

XIII	*A Dinner in Tijuana*	122

Index 128

Perkins in 1953 on his retirement.

Introduction
GUARDING THE GATEWAYS

★ CLIFFORD ALAN PERKINS, *who retired to Southern California after a distinguished career with the Immigration Service and the Border Patrol, was a small-town Wisconsin boy who had no idea as he approached the age of twenty what life had in store for him. He was hoping to go to college and had private dreams of becoming a professional baseball player. Then a suspected case of tuberculosis made it necessary for him to seek a drier climate, and he was soon on the train to El Paso, Texas, where he had relatives. After two years of boredom as a post office employee, he joined the Immigration Service as a Chinese Inspector with instructions to proceed at once to Tucson, Arizona.*

This adobe village seemed to him at first to be "some sort of jumping-off place to oblivion," though he came to have a much better opinion of the place as time went on. His duties included detection, apprehension and deportation of the flood of illegal aliens, particularly Chinese, coming across the Mexican border. In 1912 he was transferred to Douglas and in 1913 he was moved back to El Paso.

The Mexican Revolution was in progress by this time and a few months after his arrival on the Texas-Mexican border, Villa took possession of Juarez. Perkins became the official liaison man between the American officials and the Revolutionary leaders and was in almost daily contact with the General. His recollections of men and events in the fall and winter of 1913 are particularly vivid and interesting.

Regardless of, or because of, the Revolution, the smuggling of illegal aliens went on constantly. The inspectors were continually in action and often in danger. When prohibition arrived, the dangers and difficulties were multiplied. Some good men died, and many others had narrow escapes.

In 1924 the Border Patrol officially took over the activities of officers in the Outside (Chinese) Division and Perkins was promoted to command of the group. Two years later, in June of 1926, he be-

came Chief Patrol Inspector of the San Antonio Division, where a thorough shakeup was needed. That job well done, he accepted a transfer to San Ysidro, California, as Inspector in Charge. He continued there, with time out for six years as a Naval Intelligence officer during World War II, and he retired in 1953 as Chief of the Office of Immigration and Naturalization at San Ysidro.

His work in California required a special set of talents. He was now a top flight administrator and an unofficial diplomatic representative of his government. Part of his job was making friends with influential men in northern Mexico, attending ceremonial functions, and building good will. His problems were still many and serious, but he was no longer in much danger of being shot and he was able to pursue some of his hobbies, such as hunting and working with race horses. His success in meeting the demands of his last tour of duty was recognized by his Mexican friends and associates on his retirement at a celebration described in the final section of this book.

Twenty years later, when he was in his eighties, he yielded to the urging of his family and began working on his reminiscences. Nancy Dickey of Los Angeles was called in to take it all down and put it all together, finding her association with Mr. Perkins a "rare and fascinating privilege." The result was a 600-page manuscript, completed in 1974. The Tucson chapters were condensed and published as an article titled "Reminiscences of a Chinese Inspector" in the Journal of Arizona History, *17 (Summer, 1976).*

Subsequently C. L. Sonnichsen, editor of this journal, convinced that Captain Perkins' border experiences were too interesting and too valuable historically to remain in manuscript, undertook to edit them and prepare them for publication. The first problem was what to leave out. Since the story was first intended for the Perkins family, a great deal of personal material seemed expendable. Two of Mr. Perkins' three marriages were terminated, most distressingly for him, by death. Pages devoted to these tragedies and to the growing up of his two children were omitted, as were accounts of his extracurricular activities such as training and racing horses. In order to bring the book closer to reasonable length, the chapters devoted to his California years were also set aside and pages here and there were omitted or condensed. The book which emerges from this editorial reshaping is a unique and valuable document which throws much light on special aspects of border history.

Any member of the Service which guards the gateways to Mexico becomes, from the nature of his job, a repository of good stories and lively anecdotes. Mr. Perkins saw as much of human nature, had as many narrow escapes, and made as many difficult decisions as anyone in his business; his gifts as a narrator are evident in his book. He was also a thoughtful man who reflected on the history and significance of the Service to which he contributed so much. From now on, anyone interested in the Mexican border will need to familiarize himself with the recollections of Clifford Alan Perkins.

Mr. Perkins' health failed in the fall of 1977, about the time his book was being set in type. He saw the galley proofs and he hoped to hold the published volume in his hands, but his wish was not granted, for he died on December 21 at his home in Chula Vista, California — almost seventy years after his introduction to the Southwest in the border town of El Paso, Texas. It was a satisfaction to him, however, to know that his part in shaping the history of the Border Patrol would become a part of the record.

C. L. SONNICHSEN
Arizona Historical Society
January, 1978   *Tucson, Arizona*

Arizona border in 1935. The road in this picture was decided to be on Arizona's side of the boundary. Monument #189 was on the slope of the hill at the right. Tinejas Mountains show in the background.
[SMITHERS COLLECTION, HUMANITIES RESEARCH CENTER
THE UNIVERSITY OF TEXAS AT AUSTIN]

A Mexican fiscal *stands in Sonora, Mexico and shakes hands with a U.S. Border Patrolman standing in Arizona, U.S.A. at Monument #157, view to the northwest, near Sonoyta, Sonora. Picture made in 1935.*
[SMITHERS COLLECTION, HUMANITIES RESEARCH CENTER
THE UNIVERSITY OF TEXAS AT AUSTIN]

TUCSON

Jeff Milton in 1935 in Tombstone, Arizona. In 1883 he resigned from the Texas Rangers to become a U.S. Immigration Border Guard, the forerunner of the Immigration Riders. As a Texas Ranger in Capt. Charles L. Nevill's famous Frontier Battalion Company, he served many years in the Big Bend. As an Immigration Border Guard he served on the Arizona boundary and also performed the duties of a U.S. Customs official. He was known as a "one man Border Patrolman." In 1936 the Immigration and Border Patrol dedicated their latest patrol board as the Jeff Milton in San Francisco, California.

[SMITHERS COLLECTION, HUMANITIES RESEARCH CENTER
THE UNIVERSITY OF TEXAS AT AUSTIN]

I

GETTING STARTED

MY LIFE ON THE MEXICAN BORDER began with my arrival in El Paso, Texas, in 1908. To a young man from a small Wisconsin farming community with a suspected case of tuberculosis, disappointed in his hopes for a college education and a career in professional baseball, it was a strange and wonderful place. I knew nothing about the people of Mexico, whose history, language and customs were to be so deeply interwoven into the fabric of my life and I was totally unprepared for some of the experiences that were ahead of me, but I was fascinated by what I saw.

El Paso was a lusty, brawling boom town of considerable importance. As the trading and service center for practically all of West Texas, New Mexico, Arizona and northern Mexico, a steady flow of people and considerable merchandise moved in and out of the city by rail from Union Depot and the warehouses and manufacturing plants served by spur tracks along the Rio Grande. The sizeable business district had blocks of impressive buildings occupied by regional as well as local firms, plus city, county and federal offices, and there were half a dozen or more five, six and seven-story structures, including the Paso del Norte Hotel, which carried the original name of El Paso and was the best of the overtaxed hostelries in town. Most of the principal streets were paved and were jammed with busy pedestrians plus a variety of conveyances. Taxis and privately owned automobiles were not an uncommon sight, though horse drawn vehicles predominated, and a good electric streetcar system operated throughout the city. One line looped across the river to the Juarez race track. Another provided service to Fort Bliss, a few miles northeast of town, and a third ran west to the smelter district.

The more substantial of El Paso's forty thousand-plus residents, divided almost equally between Anglos and Mexicans, solidly supported the "good things of life," including a succession of legitimate plays at the Crawford Theatre, an outdoor summer stock company, and a few select but powerful civic, social and fraternal organizations. The less respectable element, plus a constantly shifting population of soldiers, gunslingers, cowboys, outlaws, peddlers, gamblers, merchants and men "heading west," patronized the gaming tables and racetrack across the river and enabled thirty or more El Paso saloons, twenty-odd gambling halls, and numerous honky-tonks and brothels to do a thriving business around the clock.

The transition from Western border town to modern city touched off a series of "Old West" killings about the time I arrived. Among those who succumbed were Deputy Sheriff Mannie Clements, who had been mixed up with the smuggling of narcotics and Chinese; former Customs Collector and sheriff Pat Garrett; saloonkeeper Tom Powers; and Tom's brother Pat, who collected the "fines" which kept the girls in the red-light district in business. Killings were commonplace and killers were rarely convicted. A man who shot to protect the sanctity of his home was nearly always acquitted, and in saloon gunfights the survivors commonly got off on a plea of self-defense. The dead man had reached into his pocket and was suspected of going for his pistol. Anyone with a cold was best advised to let his nose run and not reach for a handkerchief.

Mae Palmer Adams was another whose death contributed to the passing of an era. Mae operated the Palmer House, the biggest and best of the four parlor houses in the red-light district. Her demise hastened the closing of the district, for none of her competitors could quite fill her shoes. She ran her establishment with a sure hand and had a flair which no other madam seemed able to duplicate. She was particular about the girls she hired, insisting that they be well mannered as well as attractive, and she promoted them regularly in the downtown area on Saturday afternoons. In good weather Mae would rent a tallyho from the local livery stable, and her Negro driver, in a colorful uniform, would take seven or eight of her best-looking girls on a shopping tour, ostensibly to buy clothing but in reality to drum up business. Without Mae, the district lost its strongest and most respected advocate.

As soon as I recovered from the effects of the long train trip south, I started hunting for work, but found it a discouraging process. Nobody seemed to be interested in hiring an inexperienced, nine-

Getting Started 3

teen-year old semi-invalid, at least until I applied at the post office. Wages were higher in El Paso than in the rest of the country, but the post office was able to pay its clerks only fifty dollars a month and was having trouble filling an opening in the registered mail division. Regulations required that items held over night had to be kept in a vault, and the clerk who closed the vault at night had to be the same person who opened it the next morning. This meant that one registry clerk had to work a split shift from four to eight in the evening and from six to ten in the morning. These hours suited me perfectly, for they enabled me to rest during the middle of the day.

Since I had passed an examination in Wisconsin and my civil service rating was transferable to El Paso, the details were taken care of almost before I could think about the work required, and within days I was behind a counter writing up receipts for most of the packages passing through the post office. The work was monotonous and time consuming. It was not long before I found myself putting in well over eight hours a day. The split shift left me little time for socializing and the salary did not leave much spending money. I finally popped off one day about being sick and tired of my job to May Brick, the middle-aged spinster who relieved me at the registry window.

May looked me up and down. "If I were a young man your age," she said, "I'd get a job with the Immigration Service."

I had never heard of the Immigration Service. "What is that?" I asked her.

"It's a branch of the government," she replied, and went on to explain that it dealt with immigration, exclusion, deportation and expulsion of aliens. Most of its officers worked on the east and west coasts and on the Canadian and Mexican borders. The starting salary was more than twice what I was making. That was enough for me. I signed up the next time an announcement appeared on the post office bulletin board concerning a civil service examination for Immigration Service positions on the Mexican border. I picked up two pamphlets on immigration laws and Service regulations and started pumping Inspectors at the line and in the office for all I was worth. On schedule I took the test — then waited six anxious months for notice that I had passed and another eight months before I received notification of my appointment.

Meanwhile my work in the registry division seemed increasingly monotonous and confining. About the only interesting part of my job turned out to be the hours between four and six when the girls from the red-light district came in. Their day began at dusk, but because of the contemptuous manner in which they were treated by the clerk on the day shift, I got to know a number of them. My initial reaction was surprise, for there was nothing to distinguish them from other El Paso women except the Broadway addresses on the registered mail they sent out and picked up. They all responded to friendliness and sincerity. As more and more of them showed up during my shift, I learned to see them as individuals and to know something of the lives they led. One or two were obviously at the end of their rope. Several resented the trap in which they found themselves. Others enjoyed what they were doing — in about the same proportion as people in other professions. All of them had long ago accepted the fact that prostitution was the only way in which they could support themselves.

While waiting for my appointment to come through, I enrolled in a Spanish course at the business college for an hour a day, five days a week, at the suggestion of a new friend in the Immigration Service. Little did I anticipate that I would come to use that language as readily as English and on occasion serve as an interpreter.

On December 28, 1910, more than a year after taking the examination, I finally received notice of my appointment as a Chinese Inspector, with instructions to proceed immediately to Tucson, Arizona. I did so at once, taking the overnight Pullman to my new station, arriving early on a frosty winter morning at the old two-story gray stucco station.

For the largest city in Arizona Territory, Tucson did not strike me at the outset as amounting to much. After more than two years in El Paso, which was three times its size, the more I saw of it, the more I felt that Tucson was some sort of jumping-off spot to oblivion. The entire town, with all of its thirteen thousand inhabitants, looked as if it might dry up and blow away in a hard wind. Flat topped one-story adobe buildings, plastered a mud brown or a dirty white, edged property lines and narrow, rutted streets surrendered identity in the outskirts to an arid, sunbaked desert. A small Chinatown appeared to be developing near a joss house and half-naked children played happily in the littered cartways of the Mexican section. On my approach they watched shyly or disappeared into one-room earthen floored adobe shacks seemingly held together by each other, or shelters made from mud daubed twigs and ocotillo branches stuck into the ground and roofed over with old boards, pieces of rusted galvanized iron sheeting, and occasionally with a thatch of palm fronds.

Downtown I saw tailored businessmen, casually attired ranchers and a few well-dressed housewives keeping appointments or viewing the latest merchandise on display in the stores. Mexicans wearing loosely cut cotton pants and jackets, sandals and large sombreros meandered along South Myer Street exchanging pleasantries while their *rebozo*-covered wives made small purchases in Chinese and Mexican operated stores.

I sat down in one of the high-backed chairs in the lobby of the Santa Rita Hotel and was fascinated at what seemed the overly formal manner in which people were eating in the dining room. It was my first exposure to tables served without commotion by more than one waiter, with napkins pleated into fans, long white tablecloths, individual service plates, and more forks, knives and spoons at each place than I could conceive any use for.

This reminded me that I should be doing something about finding a night's lodging. I picked up my suitcase at the depot and before long was installed in the cheapest hotel room I could find — a second-floor single room with no heat at the opposite end of the hallway from the only bathroom.

Promptly at eight o'clock on Monday morning, I reported to the Immigration and Naturalization Service office in the two-story brick building across from the courthouse and learned that the documents covering my appointment had not been received. It took two more days for my papers to catch up with me, and I spent the interval learning more about my new home.

In spite of my initial reaction, I became more and more impressed with what had been accomplished literally in the middle of nowhere. The one, two and occasionally three-story buildings in the business district and quite a few homes in the more expensive residential section were modern and of recent construction. Also, there had to be a fair number of prosperous residents, for I saw several automobiles, although they were looked upon as curiosities rather than as means of transportation.

Tucson's commercial and professional establishments were operated primarily by Anglos, as were the firms catering to the expanding winter tourist trade and to the growing list of sanitariums built for health seekers. The restaurants and laundries, on the other hand, were operated almost entirely by Chinese brought into the country originally as laborers. Forbidden by law to own property or engage in commerce, their search for work had carried them away from the west coast. They were industrious and maintained gardens well past any area close enough to town to be considered by most citizens as desirable, and they provided most of the local residents with their fresh vegetables, chickens and eggs. Horse drawn, flat roofed wagons, with scales and brass scoops dangling from the tops, carried fresh produce, poultry and eggs to housewives every day.

These "Orientals" and their colony became a major focus of my activities a few days after my arrival.

II

THE CHINESE INVASION

※ ON JANUARY 4, 1911, I TOOK MY OATH OF OFFICE before the United States Commissioner in and for the Territory of Arizona. As it turned out, I was the last inspector appointed to enforce the Chinese Exclusion Acts.

Over the years, many laws have been passed to regulate or restrict immigration into this country. In 1875 a law was enacted prohibiting the admission of convicts and immoral women; another in 1882 sought to exclude idiots, lunatics and paupers. The Literacy Act of 1917 required that immigrants be able to read and write in some language, and the 1921 Quota Law limited the annual entry of immigrants to a percentage of those individuals of the same nationality who were here in 1910.

All laws controlling immigration discriminate against somebody and put pressure on inadmissible persons to try to enter by illegal means. Mexicans and Europeans began trying to cross the border literally by the thousands following passage of the Literacy Act and the Quota Act, but the first regulative legislation applying to persons from a particular country involved the Chinese — primarily because laborers resented competing with the many unskilled workers no longer needed by Western mines and railroads.

In 1882 the first Chinese Exclusion Act suspended for ten years the immigration of Chinese employed in mining and other skilled or unskilled occupations. This, in effect, barred the entrance of practically all Chinese, for few if any professional men were interested in emigrating from China. Those already in the country were entitled to receive from the collector of customs a certificate of identification, evidencing their legal right to go from and come to the United States.

This act was succeeded by the Act of September 13, 1888, prohibiting the immigration of all Chinese except officials, teachers, students, merchants or travelers for pleasure. Laborers who had returned to China were forbidden to reenter unless they had wives, children or parents in the United States, property therein valued at $1,000, or debts of like amount due them and pending settlement.

As a matter of practice, few Chinese who left the country tried to qualify for reentry. If they had a fairly good stake here and wanted to go back to China for a visit, they just went. Legally, they could not return without a certificate of identification, so those who did come back shipped to Mexico and were smuggled into the country with the idea of making our government prove they had been away. They even concealed their right names when they left for China so it would not be possible to establish by a ship's passenger list that they had gone.

In October, 1888, all certificates of identity were declared void and of no effect, legally eliminating any possibility of reentry. This was followed in 1893 by an act which required every Chinese in the United States to apply within six months to the collector of internal revenue for a certificate of residence and to carry it at all times. The certificate bore a photograph as well as a detailed identification of the individual and was to be surrendered if and when he left the country.

The second and final Chinese Exclusion Act, passed in 1902, prohibited the immigration of all Chinese and persons of Chinese descent until otherwise provided by law. The "otherwise" did not come to pass until 1943, when immigration restrictions for Chinese were liberalized.

During the time that these progressively restrictive measures were being passed, word was reaching men in China that it was possible to accumulate in the American West "fortunes" (by Chinese standards) of several thousand dollars. This caused a corresponding increase in the number trying to get into the country surreptitiously. All who came wanted to make enough money to return home and marry, if they did not already have wives there, live out their remaining years in what would be relative luxury, and be buried properly. They had no intention of staying in the United States permanently, and families of numerous men who died here eventually made arrangements to have their bones shipped back to China, for it was believed their souls would not be at peace so long as their remains were interred in other than Chinese soil.

Prior to the Act of February 14, 1903, which charged the Secretary of Commerce and Labor with responsibility for the apprehension of aliens, this function was carried out by the Customs Service, which had a patrol whose members were referred to as line riders. These men travelled between ports of entry on horseback with a packhorse and could stay out for a week to ten days in comparative comfort. They were charged with preventing the smuggling of anything into the United States, but their principal duty was to prevent the illegal entry of cattle, since there was a heavy protective tariff to keep them out.

Responsibility for dealing with illegal aliens was assumed by the Immigration Service in 1908 with the creation of a section called the Chinese Division, officers being designated as Chinese inspectors. The Customs Service line riders, however, having had jurisdiction for so long and being on the job, continued to pick up any suspects they ran into. Until that patrol was abolished, the two services always cooperated in the enforcement of federal statutes.

Chinese inspectors and Immigrant inspectors, working with Customs line riders, made it increasingly difficult for Chinese to get into the country via busy ports and populated areas, and as a result smuggling activities shifted to the sparsely inhabitated sections of southern New Mexico, Arizona and California. By the time I joined the Service, few Chinese were coming in east of El Paso. Some continued to enter through gulf and west coast ports, but by far the greatest numbers were entering in the vicinity of towns on or near the Mexican border and, for a while, through Canada. This border phase of law enforcement, carried on by a comparatively small number of inspectors working twelve to fifteen hours a day, seven days a week, continued until about 1917, when the Service was faced with new problems arising from the passage of the Literacy Act.

After 1893 every Chinese alien was required to carry identification, including a photograph. Such procedures invariably led to forgeries and duplications. Photography in 1893 was rather rudimentary, and many pictures on certificates of residence faded with time. Also, most of the Chinese who were required to register were adults, since the immigrants up to that point had consisted almost entirely of males over twenty-one years of age. Eighteen to twenty years later, it was almost impossible to be sure the photograph on a certificate of residence was of the person presenting it. Copies of the originals, with photographs, were supposed to have been filed in the office of the U.S. collector of internal revenue of the district where the application was made, but records were sketchy. Additionally, the forms varied from one locality to another, so the fact that one document did not look exactly like another meant very little.

When a man in his forties to mid-fifties appeared in one of Tucson's Chinese establishments, it was fairly easy for us to ascertain that he was a new arrival from Mexico since we had records of all Chinese entering by train. There was very little travel except by train, and our record books already contained the names and addresses of all local Chinese residents. Proving he came from Mexico following an unlawful trip to China, however, was more difficult, for some recent arrivals went to great lengths to hide the illegality of their entry. We had cases where the description contained in the certificate presented by a man picked up for questioning indicated that the possessor had certain scars. In one or two instances we were able to prove that the holder of the certificate was not the individual who had originally applied for it, and that his scars had actually been added so his appearance would conform to certificate details.

It was important to prove that a suspect picked up coming into the United States after a trip to China had actually been out of the country and was here illegally. Of course when he was apprehended at Tucson, Phoenix, or some other point near the border and was suspected of having just reentered the country from Mexico, he was thoroughly searched and his clothing was examined. In some cases identifying marks were found, but the Chinese soon learned to remove all such markings. Strangely enough, it was sometimes possible to trap them by making a casual comment to them in Spanish. This they might answer unthinkingly, though they would not respond to questions put to them in English. This was not prima facie evidence, but it often served as a lever to cause a suspect to confess where he had been.

For a time the Service hired Mexicans in Nogales, Sonora, to photograph Chinese on their arrival by train from the south and, if possible, to take pictures of new arrivals living in Nogales. Such pictures were supplied to the Tucson and other border Immigration offices, where they were filed by approximate age, shape of face, and body type. This reference material was often useful in establishing the fact that apprehended Chinese had been in Mexico as recently as a few weeks or months previously.

We also arranged to have pictures taken in Tucson of persons suspected of illegal entry from Mexico and sent to ports and agents on the border for referral to residents and officials in or near Mexico. In a number of instances we were able to secure witnesses who could swear in court that the alien had been in Mexico on a certain date. Bringing witnesses in from Mexico to testify in court had to be discontinued after a couple of years, however; they got to making a good thing of it since they received money to cover their expenses up and back. Their credibility suffered when one witness identified our Chinese interpreter, maintained in the office full-time by the Service, as a man he had seen getting off a train in Mexico.

The Chinese apprehended while I was in Arizona were all males, and usually in one of two age groups: young men in their late teens to twenties and old men who had lived here at one time, registered, and gone back to China without reporting their departure. Those who had been here before could usually print their names and carried their old papers, knowing that once they reached San Francisco or one of the larger inland cities with a sizeable Chinese colony, no one would be able to prove they had ever left the country. To avoid deportation, younger men had to claim they had been born here and prove it in court if they were picked up, which was relatively easy for several years if they were brought in by a corporation known as the Chinese Six Companies.

At the turn of the century this organization was one of the richest in the world. With head offices in San Francisco, the members engaged in all sorts of importing and exporting and were reportedly behind the white slave trade as well as the smuggling of opium and Chinese. As I understood their procedure, if a Chinese here had a relative or friend for whom he was willing to pay to have brought from China, he got in touch with the local representative of the Chinese Six Companies. The individual's name would be passed to the Company agent in, say, Shanghai, while the relative or friend living here would notify him to go to Shanghai. The Six Companies also brought in many young men to work for Chinese already established here. These aliens were expected to repay the Company for their expenses, which amounted to several hundred dollars, and many a so-called tong war in which Chinese hatchmen left mute evidence of their existence was merely the result of some alien's attempt to run out on his debt to the Six Companies. Often the killing was not sanctioned by any tong, but by arranging for it to appear so, the killer could easily place responsibility elsewhere.

An alien brought in by the Six Companies was given preliminary instruction in English and deportment in China, after which arrangements would be made for him to be taken to Mexico, usually aboard a Chinese ship destined for Mazatlan, Guaymas or Manzanillo. On arrival, he would be met at the docks by a Company agent who would take him in tow and see that he was put to work in a restaurant or laundry. There he could be weaned further away from some of his Chinese mannerisms and learn something of the business in which he would eventually be working. When his indoctrination was completed, he would be put on the train for Nogales, Sonora. From that city he would travel by stage (later by bus) to Naco, Agua Prieta or possibly Mexicali. There he would be turned over to a Mexican hired to take him across the border and deliver him to a contact in some nearby American town. In the United States his Americanization was continued. He would also memorize a complete description of the house where he supposedly had been born and an account of who his parents were, who the neighbors were, who lived upstairs and down, the school he attended, the names of his teachers, and the names of children he could claim to have played with — all individuals who could establish their identity in this country.

The San Francisco earthquake and fire in 1906 destroyed all records in the city hall and in all of Chinatown, so most of the younger Chinese aliens claimed to have been born there. The Six Companies management was well aware that government representatives would be unable to prove otherwise if the alien was properly trained, schooled in his cover story, and suitably dressed. If by some chance the alien was picked up, then released on bail pending a deportation hearing, the Company would arrange for delays in the hearing while he was given clothing and additional instruction. A year or so later, when he appeared in court, he would be very Americanized. Witnesses, including a few Anglos, would be brought in from San Francisco to swear he was the child born to Mr. and Mrs. So-and-So, who lived in the apartment next to them, and it would be almost impossible to disprove their stories. This procedure became so widespread that the Service stopped bothering to file charges against Chinese aliens. In the end, inability to prove they were illegal entrants made citizens out of them. At one time it was estimated that if all of those who claimed to have been born in San Francisco had actually been born there, each Chinese woman then in the United States would have had to produce something like 150 children.

To enforce laws applicable to the admission of aliens and to supervise border crossings, Immigration officers known as immigrant inspectors were and are stationed at major coastal and border sea and air ports, at rail terminals, and along vehicular access routes to inspect all incoming traffic. They also maintain surveillance of backcountry areas according to the possibility and probability of encountering illegal entrants, for the number of persons trying to cross into this country is so much greater than the force attempting to prevent them from doing so that officers must concentrate their efforts where they can do the most good. They depend for their high degree of success upon knowledge of people's habits and instinctive reactions to certain circumstances, familiarity with local topography and transportation facilities, and the fact that they are trained and equipped to survive in unexpected and potentially serious situations.

Border Patrolmen in the Arizona desert huddle around fire.
[SMITHERS COLLECTION, HUMANITIES RESEARCH CENTER
THE UNIVERSITY OF TEXAS AT AUSTIN]

III

ON DUTY

✱ THE IMMIGRATION OFFICE IN TUCSON was established to handle the apprehension, detention and deportation of aliens picked up by officers stationed at Nogales, Naco and Douglas. The primary duty of the Tucson officers was to inspect all westbound Southern Pacific passenger and freight trains and all trains arriving from Nogales, Sonora. They also carried out occasional scouting details in the surrounding country to pick up aliens reportedly moving overland. Except for Walter Miller, who was a local boy, and John Harne, a former United States cavalry officer, few of the inspectors were suited to an outdoor life and many could not even ride a horse. As this was true of most of the inspectors stationed along the Mexican border, it proved increasingly difficult as time went on for them to accomplish the amount of work involved in scouting and horseback details, so the Service began recruiting officers called mounted watchmen and mounted inspectors — the beginning of what would become the Border Patrol.

The authorized force in Tucson under Inspector-in-Charge Alfred E. Burnett at the time I joined the Service consisted of nine Immigrant inspectors, one Chinese inspector, a Chinese interpreter, two male clerks, a matron and six guards, all of whom served a six month probationary period. My appointment as Chinese inspector was made to fill the vacancy created when another officer left the Service. The title made the job sound exciting, possibly dangerous, and eventually an open sesame to the mysteries of the Orient. As the newest (and youngest) appointee in the office, it very quickly came to my attention that I was low man on the totem pole and, because I had grown up with horses, qualified to be sent out on horseback details with the least amount of notice, or sleep, when I was not checking railroad cars in the freight yards. Otherwise, my duties and status were exactly the same as those of the immigrant inspectors, for it had become apparent in the years following establishment of the Chinese Division that it was not practical to have some inspectors involved only with Chinese and others only with immigrants. All subsequent appointments at Tucson and elsewhere on the border were made as immigrant inspectors, and with my first promotion my title was changed to Immigrant Inspector.

The other part of my indoctrination, which came as something of a shock, was that we were expected to provide our own uniforms and guns within thirty days after we were sworn into office. We were allowed to wear casual work clothes — soft brimmed Stetson hats and high heeled riding boots — on scouting details. Also we put on our oldest clothing and heavy soled army boots to inspect freight cars as the work was arduous, dirty, and most of the time in weather either extremely hot or bitterly cold. During the inspection of passenger trains, while working in town and in the office, however, we had to wear uniforms and carry guns although I do not recall shooting at a single person during my two and a half years in Arizona.

Our winter uniforms were olive drab double-breasted woolen suits cut along the lines of the uniform worn by U.S. Navy officers with a badge on the left breast and an olive drab cap bearing the letters USIS over an eagle insignia above the cap bill. In summer we wore similarly cut cotton shirts and trousers, but no coat. Several companies made uniforms to order for us, and a few of the men had theirs tailor-made. The badge, buttons and cap insignia were furnished, but the government did not begin supplying anything else and the Sam Brown belt did not become part of the uniform until after the Border Patrol was established in 1924.

With only ten inspectors to cover Tucson and the surrounding countryside for forty or fifty miles, we were on duty twelve to fifteen hours a shift, seven days a week, alternating from days to nights and back every two weeks. Train inspection was the most arduous work because each car in every train destined for the interior had to be checked thoroughly for Chinese. My room was close enough to the depot so when a passenger train was due I could clean up a little before putting on my uniform without wasting too much time, but there was many a day when one more change of clothing would have finished me with the Service. Sometimes, in addition to inspecting two or three passenger trains, we opened as many as three hundred freight cars on a shift, regular loaded freights usually having from fifty to sixty cars and empties as many as seventy.

Chinese attempting to reach inland cities undetected hid in every conceivable place on trains: in box cars loaded with freight, under the tenders of the locomotives, in the space above the entryway in the old passenger cars, in staterooms rented for them by accomplices, and even in the four-foot-wide ice vents across each end of the insulated Pacific Fruit Express refrigerated cars, iced or not. We also had to check the passenger cars in the depot for travelling Chinese, making a record of their names, where they had boarded, their destinations, and any documents they carried. The information was then verified with the conductors to be sure it was correct insofar as they knew it. They were familiar with our work and told us right away whenever they had seen a Chinese board the train at a small station, especially if it had been on the side of the car away from the platform or under other circumstances that might indicate he was being put aboard by smugglers.

As soon as a passenger train had pulled out and I was back in my old clothes, I took off for the freight yards, which extended for half to three-quarters of a mile east of the depot to the roundhouse and shops and would handle seven or eight trains at one time. During our inspections we were assisted by a railroad watchman who went along to open and close the heavy car doors and by a clerk who recorded the number of each seal broken on a loaded car and, after the inspection, applied another. They were also supposed to make sure we did not take anything out of the cars, although I was always too busy, hot and dirty to think much about carrying off something.

The Los Angeles-bound banana specials from Galveston gave us the most trouble. Because the railroad wanted to move them faster than regular freights, they operated on the same schedules as passenger trains and often as sections of passenger trains. Temperatures inside the twenty-five to thirty refrigerated cars in each train had to be regulated carefully; if they were once allowed to rise above a certain point, nothing could be done to keep the bananas from spoiling as the ripening fruit would generate enough heat to literally burn itself up. Each of these trains was accompanied by a "banana messenger" to prevent such an occurrence. His job was to see that proper temperatures were maintained and they all strongly resented our opening the cars, especially to inspect the ice vents through the two lift-up trap doors on top. There was no leeway in our work for consideration of temperature variations, inside or outside the cars, and as a consequence we had more than a few arguments and once or twice a knockdown, drag-out fight with a banana messenger.

It would have been easy to skip over a few cars, and one inspector was discharged for doing just that, but the government sometimes took steps to make sure we did our work properly. One plainclothes agent tied the hasps on all doors of the loaded freight cars in a train with black silk thread at a stop east of Tucson, then checked the train again in Yuma. The man who was supposed to have inspected the train in Tucson passed every car as opened and examined and recorded its number without breaking a thread.

Once in a while a government plainclothesman would hide in one of the freight cars we were due to inspect. That was a very risky procedure, however, because cargo sometimes shifted en route or during switching operations. One day I entered a car loaded with steel pipe after the train conductor told me a man was in there. Sure enough I found him lying down at one end of the car in a small space left by some short pipe. A quick jerk by the locomotive could have caused the load to move and crush the man instantly. Such methods of spying were fairly pointless since the brakemen and the firemen usually saw the agent enter one of the cars and tipped us off. Besides, it put these men in a bad position with us. No matter how we roughed them up (we were inclined to think they were not too smart or they would have been more concerned about their personal safety), reporting us was pointless because the government did not want to acknowledge what it was doing.

When we were not inspecting railroad cars or out on scouting trips, we had to check out the establishments in and around town which were operated by Chinese for "temporary guests." Eventually I reached the point where I recognized most of the 400 or so local Chinese citizens by sight, as did several of the other inspectors, and got to know rather well a few of the older men who worked in the laundry and restaurants I frequented. For the most part they led rather solitary lives and responded readily to the slightest friendly overture.

It must have been difficult for them to become more than casually acquainted with me, for they knew I was always on the lookout for any of their countrymen who might be laying over on their way to the interior. Perhaps my visits with them just never happened to coincide with the presence of an alien in the back of their shops, for they always acted glad to see me, especially after one dinner during which my cup was filled with boiling-hot tea while my attention was elsewhere. After spilling most of the cup's contents down my shirt front into my lap and jumping up in considerable discomfort, I started laughing during the blotting up that followed and from then on several waiters (and sometimes the cook) would gather near my table to observe my enjoyment of the won ton soup and the other tasty dishes. With hands clasped under aprons, or smoking what had to be chains of cigarettes, they would chatter among themselves, indicate amusement by much head nodding, wide grins and restrained, soft laughter whenever something occurred that pleased me, too.

One of our regular calls was by horse and buggy to the Chinese vegetable gardens beyond the ruins of old Fort Lowell. The men who worked in the gardens, cultivating and irrigating vegetables for local sale and use in the restaurants serving Chinese food, wore dark blue or black loose cotton jackets and pajama-type unpressed trousers, sandals and large straw hats. They looked much alike in the harsh glare of the midday sun and unless we knew them, we had to examine their papers and check them against a loose-leaf record we took with us showing the names and types of documents carried by Chinese residing or working in every establishment in town. They called their certificates "chock chee," so we would refer to them the same way when asking to examine their papers. We all picked up a few words of Chinese and sometimes they came in handy in finding out where they lived, or in asking, "Ne gu mot ming ah?" (which spelling would no doubt cause a language expert to shudder, but that is the way it sounded) to ascertain their names.

Our record books of Chinese residents were all locally prepared for the convenience of the Tucson inspectors and to assist new officers who had to take over the duty of checking for aliens and constituted more or less an up-to-date census. They were not required to be kept by any Service directive, but were logical lists to maintain of persons with whom we were in continuous contact. It was relatively easy to recognize a man when he was always seen working as a gardener. But if, a few weeks later, he was working in a kitchen as a helper, or in a laundry, the fact that he was out of place and dressed differently would make it difficult to recognize him. When we had any doubts about a man, he would be asked to produce his chock chee and we would check it and what he told us against our records. If we had no information about him or if what he said did not agree with our files, we would take him to the office for further investigation with the assistance of our Chinese interpreter. If it was found that he was not in the United States legally, he would be held in our detention quarters and arrangements initiated for his deportation.

I had been on duty only a few weeks when I came in contact with my first illegal entry. After my shift was over one morning at seven o'clock, I left the freight yards and started uptown for breakfast. Coming toward me down the street was a two-horse hack carrying two men. I paid no particular attention to it until it pulled to the curb in front of the Shanghai Low Restaurant and I saw that the two passengers were Chinese. It was most unusual for Chinese to be riding in a cab, so I walked closer. I noticed that one was expensively attired and the other was wearing a suit that had obviously been made for a much heavier man.

Following them into the restaurant, I showed my badge to identify myself and demanded to see their papers. The well-dressed Chinese claimed to own the cafe and produced a certificate of residence that had all the earmarks of being genuine. The other did not speak any English. As he had no identification and was wearing clothes of recent make which he obviously was not used to, I took him in. Chinese were so accustomed to the loose clothing they habitually wore that they stood and walked like mannequins the first few times they put on an American suit with a coat which fitted tight across the shoulders. Where an Anglo might swing his arms, and possibly put his hands in his pockets, the alien would try to pull his shoulders in and would hold his arms perfectly straight at his sides.

Chinese aliens were seldom deported to Mexico because there was no way to control their destination or their almost immediate reentry attempts. Agents of the Six Companies were so well organized in Mexico that Chinese aliens had to be deported by ship from California ports to Asia. Approximately once a month, Service details came through Tucson picking up aliens being held for deportation by offices along their route for delivery to the Immigration office on Angel Island in San Francisco Bay.

Some of our work at the Tucson headquarters, as already noted, involved expeditions on horseback into the surrounding countryside. It used to be a relatively simple matter for aliens to cross the line away from inhabited areas because people who knew the back country avoided it. The real problem faced by the Chinese, and later by people from other countries, was to reach the interior without being detected when the only rapid means of transportation was the railroad. Moving objects can be spotted at great distances in clear air by the dust they raise, a man on horseback being visible up to five or six miles. Sitting on the ground to steady our binoculars, we would scan our surroundings, sometimes studying the motion, shadow and dust raised by some unidentified object for ten or fifteen minutes since the heat waves made it hard to be sure we were looking at a horse, a cow, a small animal or a human being. To escape observation, smugglers led aliens along river washes and through brush-covered areas whenever possible. Much of the year, small patches of grass could be found at the bottoms of the arroyos or in the low spots between hills where any available moisture would accumulate from rains higher up in the mountains. If the wash was large enough, there would also be a few pools of water, making such locations highly desirable as camp sites in an arid land. Chinese coming into the country followed the dry washes until they flattened out and disappeared before they struck out across open country to pick up the trail towards Phoenix.

In a country where water was not readily available and temperatures were often high enough to endanger survival, anyone avoiding places of habitation was assumed to be a smuggler or an alien. Reports from men working on the railroad, outlying ranchers, and the Papago Indians (who seemed to have a natural antipathy for Chinese) were our best sources of information about the movement of aliens.

Loaning horses was a custom of the country, there never being a question of pay for their use or when they would be returned. A borrowed mount could be ridden as far as necessary, swapped for another, and another; as a result, our details were not hampered by lack of stamina of the livery stable horses on which we had to start out. Most of the ranchers, on seeing our credentials, would have their remudas brought in and give us the choice of what they had, with the possible exception of their own and their family's personal horses. Nor could we ever pay for the meals they served us. It was enough to share a drink with the owner, if we had a bottle in our saddlebags, or buy him one when he came to town.

Scouting the country south of Tucson, we rode into the King Ranch late one afternoon. It was unusually well equipped, and had a main house that was luxurious for that area. Dismounting and tying our horses to the hitching rail, we walked up to the main house to discover that everyone was gone except Mrs. King. When we inquired if she had seen any Chinese passing through, she rather hesitantly said, "No," but followed her reluctant response with a cordial invitation to stay for dinner. She had our horses taken care of while we were cleaning up and she offered us the use of her husband's razor since we never carried them on scouting trips and were usually rather scruffy looking after three or four days.

Toward sundown her husband rode in on a large chestnut stallion. When he walked in the house, she immediately called him to another room and shut the door. He came in to greet us a few moments later. Laughing, he apologized for his wife. She told him that about an hour before we arrived three Chinese had passed by some distance from the ranch house. She had not told us when we inquired because she felt sorry for them and did not want to be the one responsible for their being caught.

We sat down to a wonderful dinner that evening, served with Mrs. King's best dishes and silverware on a damask linen tablecloth. We spent the night, too, going on our way the next morning after another fine meal. In the long run, everything worked out well, for we located the Chinese we were after hiding in a railroad culvert a few miles north of the ranch.

Entering the United States by wagon or on foot through that country was a hazardous, lonely proposition, and must have been a bewildering experience to the majority of Chinese who made the attempt. They had made a long and no doubt miserable ocean voyage; they had to learn a new language, become proficient at unaccustomed work in a foreign land, adapt to different customs, clothing and surroundings. About the time things became familiar, the aliens would be put aboard a mechanical conveyance they probably had never seen before. It would carry them north through uninhabited, barren and sometimes mountainous country and leave them in a sun-baked town of drab adobe buildings.

Nobody wanted them; few people made any attempt to understand them; and detection would make futile all of the effort and money expended. Mexican railroad section hands seldom would help them because they did not want anyone around who might get them in trouble; the native Indians seemed to resent their passage through the harsh land; and uniformed officials who knew the country were sent out on horseback with guns to catch them. It was little wonder so few of the Chinese we apprehended gave us trouble and so many appeared to be almost glad they were going to be sent back to China. Often it was hard not to feel sorry for some of them, even though enforcing immigration laws was our job. They had come so far, and their wants were so few in a land of so much opportunity. I did not know it then, but there would be many times when I would be caught between the natural inclination to help another human being and my responsibilities as an officer, and guided by the conviction that it is far easier not to take the first wrong step than the second.

This was one of many lessons I learned in Arizona. I had begun to evaluate people as individuals and to accept them for what they were, not for the way they looked. My judgment and awareness had been tuned up considerably. For the rest of my career in the Immigration Service I built on the foundation laid in those early years.

In September of 1912 I was transferred to Douglas, southeast of Tucson on the Mexican border. At first I thought someone must have made an administrative error. The existing force at Tucson was pushed to the limit and there appeared to be very little need for a Chinese inspector at Douglas. Chinese aliens seldom attempted to enter the country there, since there was no direct connection with the interior of Mexico and no through transportation to the West Coast. Of course it was a port of entry and I have since realized that the purpose in sending me there was to familiarize me with the routine of ports. Since it was a small facility, I was called on to perform all phases of the work.

Douglas itself was a moderately busy community of almost seven thousand people. It had been organized by the Phelps-Dodge Copper Company and the Calumet and Arizona Copper Company to serve the mines in the mountains at Bisbee, some twenty miles to the west, where no flat land was available for smelters. The population was largely Anglo, but a few Mexican families lived between the line and center of town, and there was a large settlement just outside the northwest city limits known as Pirtleville. Many of the Latins were related to the residents of Agua Prieta, a small pueblo located a quarter of a mile south of the border. Shoppers and farmers from Agua Prieta, Mexican ranchers selling cattle to the slaughterhouse east of Douglas, and a few tourists riding the north and southbound trains kept us fairly busy. Our entire force consisted of Inspector-in-Charge Frank Heath, Antonio Sierra (the interpreter) and me. We maintained regular office hours Mondays through Fridays. Sierra and I manned the port on Saturday afternoons and Sundays. The duty was light, and, with occasional horseback patrols of the line, it was a welcome change from the fifteen-hour shifts I had frequently put in at Tucson; it also provided me an excellent opportunity to learn administrative procedures. The job would have been peaceful — even monotonous — except for one thing: the Mexican Revolution.

There was little peace in Douglas after 1910, when the trouble broke out. Under the dictatorship of Porfirio Díaz, Mexico was owned almost entirely by a few immensely wealthy families who kept the rest of the people in illiterate peonage. Some landowners looked after their workers' simple needs, but the majority of the *hacendados* lived in luxury while the rest of the population struggled for bare subsistence. The discontent of the people was widespread and many Mexicans came to the conclusion voiced by the revolutionary leader, Emiliano Zapata; "It is better to die on your feet than live on your knees."

In the rough country of northern Sonora and Chihuahua, the *federales* were not anxious to tackle the roving bands of outlaws who were terrorizing and robbing the people. Groups of rebellious peons would join first one band, then another, starting out on their own as soon as they had accumulated enough equipment. They would rob, burn and kill until a larger band got after them, then join the opposing, larger band for protection.

With all the destruction, countless dispossessed residents crossed the line at Douglas, seeking refuge in the United States. Among them were a number of Mormons who had settled in western Chihuahua near the Sonora line, after leaving Utah and northern Arizona because they did not want to give up polygamy. Through their industrious efforts, they had done well, but the bandits moved in and took over their farms, stealing and destroying until they had nothing left except the clothes on their backs and what little they had been able to conceal from the raiders. Most of the Mormons arriving at the line were on foot, their meagre possessions and food supplies packed in covered wagons drawn by four-horse teams. Practically every man was accompanied by several women and numerous children, but when we questioned each we would be told this woman was his wife, that one was his sister, whose husband was still in Mexico, another was his sister-in-law, her husband was still in Mexico, and so on. Certain children would be claimed as his, some would be indicated as the sister's, others the sister-in-law's, while all of the women and the children probably were his.

With the feeling of nationalism that began to grow out of the successes of the revolutionists came a wave of general resentment against all foreigners. When this was mixed with greed, and tequila, the Chinese shopkeepers, who could be found in practically every town in northern Mexico, soon became the object of widespread persecution. Their shops were destroyed and they were robbed, beaten, and sometimes killed. Destitute and frightened, they fled into the United States to escape the terrorism, hoping to be picked up by the Immigration Service and deported to their homes in China. Wherever they could, they crossed the border and walked along roads or railroad tracks until they were seen and reported to the nearest Immigration Service office. These "free trippers" came in such numbers (until the political situation stabilized somewhat) that the cost of taking them into custody and deporting them posed a serious problem to our government.

Ranchers in northern Mexico who were able to do so moved their families north across the line temporarily, many of them from western Chihuahua and Sonora coming to Douglas. One northern Sonora ranch owner with whom I became well acquainted was Don Francisco Elías, who later became Mexican consul in El Paso and governor of the State of Sonora. He was a rather tall man, clean shaven and of medium complexion, who was friendly and very accommodating but also suave and polite. He wore American-style clothing and looked like any other well-dressed man in town, never appearing in the tight pantaloons, jacket and big hat supposedly typical of Mexican *hacendados*. As did many of the large ranchers, he brought thirty or forty of his best horses across the line under bond so they would not be stolen by the outlaws, and for almost my entire stay in Douglas one of his mounts was continuously at my disposal. Don Francisco's service to his country was not unusual for people from Sonora. It was one of the most advanced states in Mexico, with more schools per capita for children and a higher educational level available than in the other Mexican states, although there was no comparison with American schools. As a result, with the exception of the Yaqui Indians who were good soldiers but mostly illiterate, the people of Sonora were better educated. Another reason that many of Mexico's leaders came from Sonora was that it did not have the system of peonage that existed in other parts of the country.

The first four or five years of the Revolution would be marked by so many fights along the Rio Grande, and in the border states of Sonora and Chihuahua, that U.S. Army Cavalry units would be detailed to patrol the line and two embargoes against selling arms and ammunition to Mexico would be put into effect by the Wilson government. A number of skirmishes were so close to the border that gunshots could be heard in Douglas. Red Lopez, who belonged to one outlaw band operating near the Line, was caught by the *federales* about 1912 and shot a few miles from Douglas, reportedly as he was trying to escape. They buried him on the spot, and for years his grave was a landmark on the road between Agua Prieta and Naco.

One afternoon, as a local member of the Board of Civil Service Examiners, I was giving a qualifying examination for Philippine Island teachers to two applicants from Bisbee. In the transmittal report that went to Washington with the examination papers there was a space for notations as to any unusual conditions under which the test might have been given. That particular report carried the comment: "A Mexican revolution is going on; there is fighting within half a mile of this office, and the sound of rifle fire is plainly audible."

Periodic scouting trips east and west of town to check the country for signs of aliens smuggling across the border seldom turned up evidence to indicate that anyone had entered illegally. Near water holes in low lying areas I would come across small bands of cattle, or find evidence of their movement, and once in a while I would pick up the tracks of a couple of cowboys, but most of the time there was little to show that man even existed in the back country north of the border. Below the line was another matter. Because of the uprisings, there was always the posibility of encountering *federales, rurales,* revolutionaries, renegades, and bandits. The first two could be expected to let me go on my way in one piece, though not without considerable humorous (to them) heckling, but there was no knowing what the rest would do, for they were about as predictable as snakes.

One day when Inspector-in-Charge Heath directed me to ride the six or eight miles west to Forest and back, I picked out a large, leggy chestnut owned by Don Francisco, as the livery stable did not have an animal I felt could make the trip. Reaching Forest along the main road, I cut south through open country with the intention of returning due east to Douglas along the border. As I rode over a low hill, I happened to glance back and saw a group of Mexicans cutting behind me, evidently planning to block my return. I did not think they would kill me if they caught up with me, but I was not particularly enthused at the thought of being stripped of my guns, horse and saddle and being forced to walk home. Judging by the direction they were riding, I figured it would be difficult to evade them, so I gradually reined my horse left as though I were swinging back in an arc toward Forest, and as soon as I was out of sight in a low spot, turned my horse around and raced south into Mexico.

It was not long before I intersected the wagon road from Naco to Agua Prieta and on more level ground put my horse into a long mile-eating lope. I kept him in that gait because I had no way of knowing what lay between me and safety, and an open gallop would have taken too much out of the horse too fast. It was just as well, for around a bend I barrelled right into the middle of what was apparently the band's far-from-deserted camp. By the time I spotted them, the outlaws were too close for me to turn back, and I knew the rest of the bunch was not far behind. Gambling on the fact that all the men I could see were squatting and sitting around talking, or apparently asleep, I jammed my spurs into Don Francisco's chestnut. Leaping forward, with me leaning low over his neck, he flattened out into a dead run right through the center of the camp.

To add to the confusion, I fired a couple of shots at random from my six-shooter. Those renegades scattered in twenty different directions, sending cooking equipment, saddles, blankets, and horses flying, one man desperately trying to pull his pants up from around his knees as he ran. Out of the corner of my eye I observed two or three of them attempting to mount fractious horses still tied to a couple of bushes, so I put the chestnut into a slow run and kept him there until we were a long way off.

The renegades' ponies were seldom very fast, for they received no care and the poor graze available gave them little energy. With a magnificent grain-fed horse under me, I had little trouble outdistancing the men attempting to catch me, and finally crossed back into the United States just west of the Nacozari branch-line tracks. It was some time, however, before I made that particular trip again without the company of a Customs line rider.

That cross-country chase was my last adventure before I was transferred to El Paso.

Two groups of Border Patrolmen. Above, at Brownsville, Texas on April 24, 1928. Below, at Laredo, Texas on April 18, 1928.

[PHOTOS FROM PERKINS COLLECTION]

EL PASO

IV

ON THE FRINGES OF REVOLUTION

★ I WAS POSTED TO EL PASO, TEXAS, effective May 15, 1913, and arrived just in time to take a hand in some stirring events. The Mexican Revolution had been under way for three years. El Paso, as the largest city on the border, was a focus of undercover revolutionary activity and Juarez, only a few steps across the International Bridge, was the scene of some heavy fighting. The Service could not help being involved, and I was involved too as the newest man on a force of over fifty people at a large and active port, headquarters for the entire border at that time.

F.W. Berkshire, the Supervising Inspector, was then in charge of the entire Mexican boundary, from San Diego to Brownsville. He was a rather large man who seldom said or did anything until he had thought it out. For some reason he took more than a casual interest in me, calling me into his office every so often, talking to me more like a father than a supervisor, especially after my temper had involved me in a bit of trouble. I never knew for sure, but from the concern he showed for my progress, I always suspected my transfer to Douglas was his idea and that he wanted to give a young officer an opportunity to show what he could do. Anyway, it turned out that way, and I still remember clearly some of the advice and help he gave me.

He had a habit of gazing intently at the person he was addressing and chewing tobacco at the same time. Without taking his eyes off his subject, he would spit toward a cuspidor beside his desk, which would signal the commencement of an unhurried summation of his deliberations. He would keep me riveted in position for several minutes, his jaws rhythmically working a chew of tobacco. After successfully ejecting an amber stream into the cuspidor, he would start in.

About the time I transferred to Texas, George J. Harris was appointed Assistant Supervising Director and thus became my immediate superior. When it became necessary for proper administration to divide the border into three districts, he became director of the El Paso District, which reached from east of Yuma, Arizona, to Del Rio, Texas.

Including the supervisory personnel, there were perhaps thirty-five officers at the headquarters. In addition, the detention quarters employed a clerical staff of about fifteen, plus three interpreters, two matrons, and a complement of guards who also manned the Stanton Street Bridge to keep people from walking in from Mexico against what was supposed to be one-way southbound traffic. In all, close to sixty people worked in and out of the two large red-brick leased structures east of the Santa Fe Street Bridge. The main building was given over to offices and had a full basement where aliens could be detained and fed pending deportation proceedings. Adjoining, and connected by a covered walkway, was a two-story detention facility capable of housing approximately twenty aliens per floor. It was a number of years before the Service occupied quarters owned by the government because there was a question as to whether the land we used belonged to Mexico or the United States. Changes in the river channel had created an area called the Chamizal, which was claimed by both nations. The question was resolved by President John F. Kennedy and arrangements were completed during the Lyndon Johnson administration for handing the disputed territory over to Mexico.

When I arrived, Pancho Villa's forces were moving northward through Chihuahua and in mid-November they occupied Juarez. As they progressed toward the border, they commandeered all railroad rolling stock, including locomotives, loading equipment onto freight cars on top of which women and children traveled and even built fires. A couple of passenger cars would be hooked on for the officers and their women, and a caboose for the train crewmen would bring up the rear. These latter worked under the guns of Villa and did only as they were told. Altogether, the train was pretty much self-contained and occasionally even included a stock car full of cattle so there would be meat for everybody.

The Villistas raised considerable hell as they progressed and a great wave of refugees poured across the line ahead of them. These frightened and often destitute people became the responsibility of the Immigration Service. They included a wide variety of human types — merchants, housewives, children, workingmen, along with prostitutes, criminals, beggars, and street scum. Villa's men enjoyed killing Chinese of all varieties, and they too fled to the United States to save their lives: tradesmen, cooks, laundrymen, and gardeners. Each fugitive brought whatever he could with him, especially food, clothing and household goods, with some miscellaneous livestock and pets.

Among the earliest arrivals, when actual fighting broke out, was the entire mounted police force in a body and in a hurry. Villa had been known to cut off one ear of a captured *federal* (for future recognition), telling him as he did so that if he ever caught him again, he would kill him. And he meant it. Provision was made for turning the horses of these *federales* over to the United States Army and placing them under guard. The men themselves were paroled to the Mexican consul in El Paso. In due time the better-known individuals and others who could establish their good character were freed on their own recognizance. The rest quickly swamped the Immigration Service.

Without available housing and feeding facilities, the government people had to put them in a temporary camp behind the railroad enbankment near the river, where Army guards could patrol the area to keep them from escaping and where field kitchens could be used to feed them. The beggars and street people were a particular problem. Mexico had not yet made provision for the care of the indigent and many of them had become beggars, often grotesquely crippled and always pathetic.

Once some semblance of order existed in Juarez, repatriation of individuals ineligible for parole was mandatory. The Service detailed me to make contact with Villa and work out arrangements. The fighting had tapered off, but gun battles were still going on in various sections of Juarez and traffic was nonexistent as I left the office and headed for the International Bridge. It was usually crowded at that hour of the morning, a streetcar on the elevated track along one side, foot traffic on the walkway along the other, and a line of horse drawn vehicles plus an occasional automobile in the center. Today it was deserted, except for one barefooted Villista in ragged pants and high-crowned straw hat with two banderillas across his chest containing not more than eight or ten cartridges. Under his supervision I crossed to the Mexican side of the river.

I was in difficulties at once. Several ragtag soldiers armed with assorted weapons quickly closed around me and my idea of walking alone through their ranks, hoping they would be more amused than upset by such temerity, began to seem more foolhardy by the second. I explained my intention of talking with *El General.* A prolonged serio-comic debate followed which ended in their drawing aside, but as I moved off, a steady stream of sneering jibes about *gringos* and American *peegs* followed me, calculated to make me mad. I would have been, too, had I not been so acutely aware of the exceedingly vulnerable area between my shoulder blades.

When I reached the customs building on Avenida Juarez, I was passed on to the Officer of the Guard and obtained his permission to proceed to Villa's command post in the police station on Calle Commercial. As I continued my progress, I encountered more soldiers, and it was not consoling to observe that they were in festive mood, for I well knew it would take very little to change bantering vulgarities to bullets. There was sporadic shooting all along Calle Commercial. The sidewalks were littered with broken glass and merchandise that had been taken or thrown out of the stores. There were more dead soldiers and horses than I wanted to count and several bullet-riddled cars and wagons had been abandoned along the gutters.

Everywhere I looked was evidence that while the officers had been appropriating the better houses for themselves and their women, the Villista soldiers had been on a drunken rampage, looting, burning and killing. Order of a sort had been restored, but more than one *soldado* leaning against the wall of a vandalized saloon, liquor store or office building, was too drunk to fire the gun he waved at me so threateningly.

About the time I started debating the wisdom of reaching my destination by some other route, a man wearing the racing commisioner's full-dress uniform staggered out of an alley. I knew him well. He was, or had been, a racetrack ticket seller who answered to the name of Luis. As this resplendent figure rounded the corner onto Calle Comercial, a loaded peon, seated in the corner doorway of a ruined liquor store, observed him. The soldier's rifle was propped against the side of the building so he more easily could consume the contents of two bottles of tequila which he had confiscated. At sight of the uniform he carefully settled his bottle between his thighs, saluted and called out, *"Hola, mi capitán!"*

Since Villa was well acquainted with the racetrack personnel, it was obvious that Luis knew his general. I realized that this could be opportunity knocking, but at the same time I wondered how Luis would react to me in his new situation. I could only wait to find out. Weaving in my direction with a bemused smile on his face and a bottle of tequila in each hand, he stopped every so often to take a drink from one bottle or the other, apparently indifferent to the occasional bullet whistling by. Within a few feet of me, he stopped, frowned uncertainly, rocked forward to search my face, then threw both arms around my shoulders with an exuberant greeting, offering me a drink from either, or both, of his bottles. Under the circumstances I was happy to accept.

On his inquiring what business brought me to Juarez, I explained that my purpose was to obtain permission from *El General* for the return of some poor people who were being held in El Paso with no roof over their heads and no food to eat. I made the story as pathetic as possible and he became increasingly sympathetic. At the conclusion he offered to go with me to the police station to make sure all arrangements were worked out immediately. When we arrived, he brushed past the guard on duty with a wave of his hand and escorted me straight to the officer of the day. As a result, a messenger was dispatched immediately to the general.

After only half an hour (though it seemed much longer) the messenger returned with the necessary clearances. The two bottles were nearly empty by then, but Luis could still move under his own power when I stood up to leave. Nor was he about to allow his good amigo to walk back to the bridge alone. He presented me with one of the bottles and put an arm around my neck as we started for the river, staggering and swaying along and singing at the tops of our voices, though mine could not have added a thing to his rendition of "La Golondrina." In the middle of the International Bridge my almost paralyzed escort bade me a tearfully affectionate farewell, made an exceedingly sloppy about face, and started back towards Juarez while I went on thankfully to the office to report a mission completed.

By the time word got around that permission had been granted by *El General* for Juarez residents to return, they had been divided into groups according to their need for detention under American statutes and the problems they, or their possessions, presented. The first group ushered back into Mexico under guard included all horses, burros, livestock and wagons. Next went the cripples, beggars, prostitutes and the rest of the human refuse that had been filling the jails. The more or less responsible refugees were allowed to move out when ready, although many of them did so reluctantly, having a good idea they would find their homes and stores in ruins. None of them displayed much emotion, although there was no food immediately available in Juarez and little water. Electricity was still shut off by the El Paso supplier, and they had almost nothing to look forward to but hardship and probably slow starvation. Residents of consequence sent servants back to check on the condition of their homes, most of which had been completely stripped or taken over by high-ranking officers, their friends, and their women, and the furnishings wrecked. Many who had suffered severe financial losses or were afraid to go back remained on the American side until notified by the Service either to return to Mexico if they wished to avoid deportation or to apply for permanent residence, a simple procedure at the time since visas were not required.

Although none of the refugees expressed any particular gratitude for the food and other provisions we made for them, and their presence posed many monumental problems, El Paso residents reaped one unanticipated benefit from Villa's triumph. That summer the Villistas had taken over control of practically the entire State of Chihuahua, had seized the treasury to get money for guns, ammunition and supplies, and had occupied many of the large haciendas.

Villa's men rounded up the cattle on the larger estates, making deals with the *hacendados* at something like five dollars a head for signing the papers legalizing sale in the United States. While the fee was tantamount to no payment at all, the owners had little choice; it was that or nothing, and trainload after trainload of cattle arrived at the line and were sold through one of the El Paso banks, Villa collecting all but the head fee paid to the owners. Slaughterhouses were set up to butcher the beef, which was sold retail or given away to the poor, probably in an effort by Villa to make himself popular with the element that represented his principal backing. El Paso residents who were in a position to do so bought Villa money, which had no real value but had to be accepted in the towns he controlled and used it to purchase meat in Juarez. The meat was every bit as good as it should have been, coming as it did from the best cattle the ranchers had been able to produce.

Almost every day while Villa held Juarez, situations arose that necessitated reaching his top command, most of them having to do with the actions of Villistas at the line. Soldiers on guard at the bridge would not pass anything or anyone on their own initiative; permissions had to be obtained for the entry into Mexico of aliens being deported; two or three times a week, at least, there was some matter which had to be cleared with Villa personally. Probably because of my successful negotiations concerning the refugees and the fact that I spoke the language, the Immigration Service assigned me to act as go-between with Villa and his officials.

The general was a chunky, powerfully built man with the slender legs of a horseman, tiny, close-set black eyes almost buried in a round, full face, and a thin-lipped mouth overpowered by a heavy, drooping black mustache. Though he seldom raised his voice and was not at all bombastic, he was extremely alert and quick; his speech as well as his manner reflected his abrupt, determined attitude towards everything and everybody. All sorts of stories have been written about the general, but in the main my personal dealings with him were very satisfactory. Sometimes it was difficult to convince him about something, but when he finally agreed, he could be depended upon. I do not know whether he was dedicated to anything more than power and fame for himself, but he ran the show and accomplished his purpose. He gave everybody trouble, but you could look him in the eye and if he was a friend, fine; if not, you had better watch yourself from then on. Villa never consulted with his officers about a matter presented to him and brooked very little interference; although he was crude, he always treated me with courtesy, shaking my hand when we met, and again when we parted, giving me a firm, hearty grip. He was a dangerous, vindictive enemy when crossed, but I found the best way to get along with him was just to stand up to him in the belief that if I dealt fairly with him, he would do the same with me. It worked out that way, too.

After several weeks of almost daily contacts with the general, just about the time conditions in Juarez appeared to be reaching a semblance of normal, somebody took a potshot at me during one of my trips to Villa's headquarters. As I passed in front of a saloon near the *comandancia*, a sudden commotion erupted around the corner; a shot rang out and a bullet shattered the saloon window right above my head. There was not time to be frightened, or at least the excitement of the situation overcame physical fear. It was the same at other times in my life when I had equally close calls; three or four hours afterward, I would let down and sometimes actually become weak. The only times when I experienced cold creeping fright was when there was time to think about the possible danger ahead.

About a week after the bullet broke the plate glass window, a Mexican Customs officer told me that a drunken Villista officer had spotted me less than ten feet away and had decided to kill himself a *gringo*. Jerking his gun, he pulled the trigger just as another Customs officer recognized me and slammed the drunk's arm upward, deflecting the bullet over my head. He also told me that when Villa heard about it, he busted the officer and put him in jail.

Villa seldom left his office in Juarez, and I do not recall ever seeing him in the United States. Not only would he have been arrested for violating our neutrality laws, but the *federales* had undercover agents in El Paso, any number of whom would have risked killing him, given the opportunity. Most of his affairs were handled through his staff, primarily by Rodríguez, his buffer, personal aide and secretary. Rodríguez was a slender, neatly dressed young man in his mid-twenties who spoke English well and had the ability to be courteous yet to screen everyone who came to see the general. Once while I was at headquarters on a routine matter, Rodríguez asked me to step into the general's office to discuss something of a confidential nature. Villa was waiting for me with a proposition.

He wanted to get around the embargo against selling munitions to forces opposing the party in power in Mexico. President Wilson had forbidden this traffic in order to cooperate with the seemingly stable government in Mexico City, thereby giving rise to considerable smuggling of guns and ammunition west of El Paso where there were few barriers to such activities. After considerable beating about the bush, Villa said that he had checked me out and decided I could be trusted to undertake a commission for him. He told me he had $50,000 in gold and wanted me to go to Canada to purchase guns and ammunition for his men, a difficult task made doubly so by the varying calibers and gauges of the guns they used. Since the general had, in a manner of speaking, paid me a compliment and was not a person who took kindly to having his requests turned down, refusing him presented a real problem. I declined, however, as gracefully as possible, but as a result we never got around to discussing what he would have paid me for the job. It would no doubt have been well worthwhile financially, as agents in such dealings usually received a kickback from the seller in addition to the commission from the buyer. Before we parted, Villa did tell me that he had given $50,000 to another American for the same purpose and had never seen the munitions or heard of the agent again. Such incidents, as well as the assistance given by our government to those the general considered his enemies, undoubtedly accounted for much of his antipathy towards *norteamericanos.*

Americans did have their place in his scheme of things, for while he held Ciudad Juarez, he insisted that Luz Corral de Villa, his legal wife as far as was generally known, spend her nights in a house he rented for her in El Paso. The general was accompanied from place to place by innumerable women and referred to several of them as his "wife." He would not have been averse to going through any number of wedding ceremonies if it suited his purpose, but whatever the status of the women with him, he did not want Luz in Juarez overnight because he anticipated an attack by the *federales* at any time.

Luz was a woman of about twenty when I first met her as I was relieving an Immigrant Inspector on the International Bridge. She dressed unpretentiously with a *rebozo* over her head and was gracious, soft spoken and very much on the quiet side, but she loved the diamonds Villa gave her and wore lots of them. Her skin was lighter than average for her people, but she was rather heavy set and there was nothing in her manner to distinguish her from any other Mexican housewife. She would leave El Paso for Juarez in the morning in a large black chauffeur-driven car, occasionally accompanied by another woman, and would return about sundown or shortly thereafter following dinner with Villa. One day I learned from a friend that a detective on the El Paso police force was planning to take Luz into custody the next evening when she returned from Mexico. His intention was to shake her down and relieve her of the diamond rings and earrings she usually wore, plus the large sum of money it was her habit to carry. The detective figured that since the United States government did not recognize Villa or his army and authority in Mexico, the general would not be able to do a thing about it, and nobody in the States would care.

As soon as I heard what was in the offing, I called Villa's office. When I got through to Rodríguez, I said, "You tell Luz when she comes over tonight to leave all her diamonds and her money in Juarez." When he wanted to know why, I answered, *"Por que sí!"* (just because). That evening when Luz' car crossed the bridge, it was stopped by two detectives. They climbed into the limousine and directed her chauffeur to drive to the police station. A friend told me several days later that the detective nearly had apoplexy when he discovered that Luz was wearing no diamonds and had only small change in her purse.

Villa returned the favor a few weeks later following a shooting on Cordova Island, 400 acres of silt deposited along the north side of the Rio Grande left as the river shifted its course farther and farther into Mexico. Trees and shrubs had found a foothold in the loose soil, offering a measure of protection from observation, especially at night. A screen of brush and cottonwoods dotted the Mexican side of the one-time riverbed, and a densely populated maze of Mexican shanties on the American side gave immediate shelter to *contrabandistas*. Smugglers gave us more trouble here than any place else in the vicinity of El Paso.

While Jack Belcher and I were patrolling the Island one afternoon, we noticed a mounted Mexican officer who forded the river and rode directly toward us. We made no effort to conceal ourselves, but when he was forty or fifty yards away, he suddenly dismounted, raised his rifle, and started pumping lead at us. We dropped to the ground immediately and returned his fire. When no more shots came from his direction, we cautiously stood up and walked toward him, finding that two of our shots had reached their mark. As we stood there reviewing what had happened, I took off my hat and discovered that one of his bullets had gone throught it. This was probably my closest call in the Service, for some of my hair, which was cut fairly short, had been clipped off and was still clinging to one of the two holes through the crown of my Stetson.

If a smuggler was killed at night and fell in the river, we forgot about the body unless it showed up downstream on the American side. Then, as with a smuggler killed north of the river in the daytime, we called the police to dispose of the remains, which was usually by burial in a potter's field, for the bodies were seldom claimed. Villa had to be notified about his dead officer, however, so Jack and I left the man there and returned to our office to report the incident before I drove to Juarez. When I reached Villa's office, I explained to Rodríguez the reason for my visit and he took me to the general. We went through our usual handshake and introductory greetings, after which I proceeded (most respectfully) to tell him that one of his officers had opened fire on us on the Island, without provocation or warning and an exchange of shots had followed. Villa was rough, but I was counting on the fact that he kept his soldiers fairly well restrained, and in some ways was strict with them. With a semimilitary force, which is what his army really was, discipline was an off-again, on-again proposition. Every once in a while a Villista with too much *aguardiente* in him would shoot off his gun at nothing in particular, but after the looting and drinking had run their course, Villa's men were surprisingly orderly. As a matter of fact, other than for a few killings, I do not remember hearing of any major crimes that took place while he held the town.

The general listened to my report with his usual frowning concentration. When I was through, he remarked briefly, "I'll take care of him immediately."

"Thank you, *mi General*," I responded, "but you do not need to do that. We already have."

With that I indicated on the map hanging against the wall where the body could be found.

"*Está bien*," was all he answered before shaking hands with me again and wishing me a good journey back to El Paso.

V

THE DAILY GRIND

★ ALTHOUGH VILLA AND HIS REVOLUTION provided a dramatic break in our daily routine, our standard problem situations were never far away. I found on my arrival that the border was as porous in Texas as it was in Arizona and that the smugglers were busily at work. The flow of Chinese aliens was even greater and we kept the detention quarters busy. My initial contribution to them came from the freight yards about eleven o'clock one night shortly after my transfer. For some time we had been aware that smugglers were receiving assistance from railroad employees, so the minute we were tipped off that aliens were scheduled to be put aboard a freight train, I went to the yards and hid under one of the cars on a siding. In about an hour, a Mexican put in an appearance with three Chinese in tow. As I watched, he concealed them under one of the knuckle racks (for boxcar couplings). When he left, I went over to the rack and crawled in with the Chinese, holding my gun on them to keep them quiet. In about half an hour a brakeman approached the rack, stopped to blow his nose in order to look around, then bent over and motioned for us to follow him. I crawled out with my gun pointed at his middle, telling him to freeze. When he had made up his mind that running was useless, I called to the Chinese, then escorted all four to free beds behind bars.

These smugglers used all sorts of tricks to defeat us. By assuming the role of bedridden or seriously ill patients, accompanied by uniformed nurses, many Chinese succeeded in reaching inland cities in the drawing rooms of passenger trains. Storage areas in other parts of the train were also used, as we learned when the body of a dead Chinese was discovered in the ice compartment of a diner while it was being cleaned in the Kansas City railroad yards. It was determined that the man had actually frozen to death.

Much of the Chinese alien smuggling was timed to coincide with the breakup of the Juarez racetrack winter meet. When the season was over, horses were shipped by rail to Chicago, New Orleans, and

The Daily Grind 45

various eastern tracks, and the potential to defray shipping costs by accommodating occasional smugglers was sufficiently enticing to require corrective measures. Usually there would be at least one whole trainload of cars containing race horses, the larger stables sending their animals by express cars and the rank and file owners using ordinary box cars. To check each car thoroughly when it was fully loaded with animals and feed for several days presented a real problem, for it involved inspecting both ends of the car where baled hay was customarily piled. One-and-two-horse owners would build a boxlike structure about three and a half feet high, with one movable board, at the end of the car behind the temporary horse stalls. On top would be loaded bales of hay, racing tack, and so forth. Underneath, men would be allowed to hide until the train was on its way.

Allowing racetrack followers to travel in these so-called sweat boxes was one thing; accommodating Chinese aliens was quite another. When we found out about it, I was detailed to the track every day during the winter meet to become acquainted. Sometimes I would go over in the morning and spend the entire day visiting around the stables, so that I became acquainted with many of the people there, including the men in the secretary's office. A certain amount of bad feeling always exists between winners and losers, and it was not difficult to find out from one what the other was doing. When it came time for the meet to break up in March, I had a good idea which owners were short of funds. The racing association would often loan established owners enough money to hire box cars for their horses, as they did not want the animals at the track when the meet was over, but men who were not well known had a real problem getting their horses out of town.

Whenever we learned that horsemen in financial difficulties were shipping out, we would go to the railroad company office and obtain the numbers of the cars they had ordered and when they were scheduled to cross the line. The customary procedure was for smugglers in Juárez to cross the Chinese over the river and convey them to some point thirty or forty miles north of the border where the trains stopped for water. There they would be loaded into the horse cars so no Chinese would be in the cars when Customs and Immigration officers inspected them at the line. Owners could make anywhere from three to five hundred dollars apiece by allowing illegal aliens to travel in their box cars, which sounded attractive to horsemen, or gyps as they were called, when they were broke. As a result of a single season's work, four parties of Chinese were apprehended and race horse owners gave us very little difficulty thereafter.

Customs assigned a new man to the International Bridge one night when I was to be on duty there, and I was asked to look after him and help him in any way possible. There was open gambling in Juarez at the time, and usually the crowds returning from the gambling halls between one and three in the morning could be counted on to stir things up one way or another. Around two o'clock, a car stopped outside the port, and when we walked out I recognized the woman driver as one of the prostitutes who played the Juarez gambling crowd. After checking her in and out several evenings, I got to the point of bantering with her about her accomplishments. Most of the time I kidded her a little about having so many customers who gave her so much money she would soon be rich enough to retire. This particular night, when I reached the car I made some remark along the lines of previous conversations, but instead of answering me in a similar vein, she swelled up and acted offended. I could think of no reason for her reaction, but while debating the advisability of making another casual comment, I happened to notice her hand on the car door. She had to be extremely nervous about something, for her fingers were beating a tattoo on the metal. That was not like her, so far as I knew, so I told the Customs officer to shake her down and give her car a good going over.

Telling her to get out, he searched the car thoroughly but could not find a thing. While he was inside the car, however, it occurred to me that a few weeks previously, when I was out hunting with a friend who owned a battery shop, he mentioned being asked to make up some half-sized batteries. He was puzzled about why anybody would want a battery that filled only half the normal-size battery box. Remembering this, I called the Customs inspector and suggested that he check the battery on her car. He did so and there was nothing unusual about it except that it was clean in a car that was well layered with dust. Then I suggested that he get a piece of wire, pull one of the battery plugs, and run the wire down into the cell. He found that the wire would go down only half as far as it should, so we pulled the battery out and cut it open. The bottom half of the box was filled with heroin.

Smugglers tried every way imaginable to bring drugs into the country, even secreting them inside their bodies. Any place large enough to conceal a small package was suspect and has probably been used for the purpose at one time or another. Apprehension of drug smugglers was a function of the Customs Service and not primarily our responsibility, but we always cooperated with their officers. It was quite educational to watch them search an automobile, and every so often we were able to put the lessons to use.

The president, one of the vice-presidents, and the cashier of the El Paso Bank and Trust Company were in the habit of lunching in Juarez during the week, and over a period of time I became friendly with them. When an American hophead found out how regularly they crossed the bridge, and where they usually ate, he started going to Juarez, buying heroin, and sticking small packages of it under the fenders of the car the bank officers used. Customs officers searched that hophead time and time again when he crossed back into El Paso but never found a thing on him, naturally. They knew he had to be getting his dope across the line somehow, so they arranged to have a Mexican tail him in Juarez, and that was how they discovered his carrier. After the Mexican reported seeing the addict hide something under one of the banker's car fenders, Customs officers were staked out in the garage where the vehicle was parked during the day, and a tail was put on the car whenever it was moved. When the addict showed up in the garage to recover his heroin, he was caught red-handed, providing all of us for some time with a topic of conversation with the bankers because of their "conspiring" to smuggle drugs into the country.

Checking traffic on the bridge and trying to communicate, usually in Spanish, with travelers speaking many different tongues, was sometimes slow going. The State of Chihuahua, for instance, had a large Japanese population, and quite a few applicants for admission at El Paso were Japanese businessmen. Their requests were often for crossing cards so they could purchase merchandise in the local stores, there being few manufacturing or processing plants in Mexico. The firms they represented and the frequency of their visits were sufficient, however, to warrant the hiring of a Japanese interpreter to handle their cases expeditiously and fairly. Most of them spoke fairly fluent Spanish, but Spanish with a Japanese accent is anything but easy to understand. A number of German-speaking people also showed up at the border when Villa chased all foreigners out of Chihuahua and Torreon. Germany had sent many young single men to Mexico in the years preceding World War I with instructions to go into business and to marry local women. By entrenching them in the country and the communities where they lived, German leaders anticipated being able to establish bases of operation close enough to the United States to divert some of our attention and war material away from Europe when they took the offensive there. We gave no more thought to those Japanese and German residents of Mexico than we did to aliens from other countries, for in the Immigration Service it is necessary to evaluate people as individuals, rather than as Germans, Japanese or Mexicans.

To do a good job, an inspector must respect and even like people and determine their admissibility according to facts and an assessment of character, rather than looks. Accent, appearance and clothing are part of the picture, of course, but applicants are sized up more by mannerisms and reflex actions, and it becomes almost second nature to take in and retain definite impressions of anything slightly out of the ordinary. The average individual cannot lie without showing it one way or another. Applicants at the line are always nervous, but indications of nervousness are expected by Immigrant Inspectors. The absence of any signs of an alien's being ill at ease, or the slightest evidence of fear, register immediately in the mind of the Inspector as suspicious and become a matter for consideration in the decision he must make. He wonders why the applicant is acting the way he does, and he begins to doubt and probe every bit of information he has gathered about this particular alien. Walking down the street one day in uniform, I picked up an illegal entrant merely because I saw him dart suddenly across the street ahead of me, right in the middle of the block. Wondering why, I gave the man a second look, then crossed the street and stopped him. Had he continued on his way toward me, I probably would have paid little or no attention to him.

The influx of Chinese aliens was stopped for all practical purposes in 1916. The border troubles with Mexico and the involvement of the United States in World War I changed the situation completely. Termination of steamship passenger service between the Orient and Mexico shut off those who intended to smuggle into the United States via Mexican ports, and most of the Chinese still residing in Mexico had to leave. Taking advantage of the Revolution, unscrupulous Mexican officials interested in acquiring something for nothing harrassed the thrifty, defenseless Chinese shopkeepers who had made themselves a major factor in the country's merchandising. Property was confiscated; some were thrown in jail and many were forcibly run out; the rest were pushed around until they were glad to leave.

The Service recognized the decreasing importance of the problem by changing my designation from Chinese Inspector to Immigrant Inspector on July 1, 1917, although my duties remained the same. As in Tucson, the office maintained loose-leaf files on all Chinese who owned and operated establishments as well as on the 500 or more Chinese in the city. Most of the men and the half-dozen or so women belonged to three substantial families: the Mars, the Ings, and the Wongs. Several of the older men were substantial businessmen and highly respected in the community, especially Chew, the oldest Mar, who operated one of El Paso's best restaurants. He was an outstanding man and a fine father who insisted that all the young Mars adopt Americanized given names so they could be remembered easily by the local residents. One Mar Ben, Mar Chew's younger brother and an excellent chef, had been legitimatized by a trip to court during his late 'teens, and Mar money was behind a number of the fifty or sixty aliens in town whom we ignored because they created no problems. Also, we were well aware that prosecution would result in legalizing their status at our expense.

As things turned out, all of these men became citizens, for they were part of an El Paso contingent which enlisted in the National Guard when Villa was in his heyday in Juarez and were blanketed into the Army when the United States declared war on Germany. Because of their outstanding military record, the Immigration Service for all practical purposes conceded their status as citizens and did not question it thereafter. Several Mars were killed in combat in Europe, and two came home with serious though not permanent injuries. One Mar Ben told me when he returned that he had not received a scratch, although a couple of stray shells ploughed up ground where he had been standing a few moments previously. For some mysterious reason known only to the Army high command, he was one cook who was properly assigned to the work he did best, and fought the war in a field kitchen.

Perhaps the best known Chinese in El Paso was a man called Charlie Sam. Though he had no legitimate business to my knowledge, he reputedly controlled Chinatown and was suspected of being behind all local smuggling of opium and Chinese. Charlie was generally known as the Mayor of Chinatown, acting as go-between in all matters involving El Paso officials and the local Chinese. Whenever one of them was arrested, he would appear promptly to arrange for bail; he contributed to various charities in the name of the Chinese colony; whenever a civic affair was scheduled which called for the Chinese to be represented, Charlie would either be there or send somebody to act for him. He was always alert to what was going on and was an extremely affable, outgoing individual. In his mid-fifties, he spoke perfect English and wore beautifully tailored, expensive suits which more than made up for his small stature. We saw Charlie around Chinatown every day, though seldom before noon, and no matter how often we kidded him about how many Chinese he had smuggled into the country the previous week, or when he had more coming in, he would smile broadly and not take offense. He no doubt realized that when we quit bantering with him, he would be in real trouble. Charlie was known as a principal in the fan tan gambling in Chinatown. He lived upstairs over an herbalist's, which was nothing more than the front for a gambling hall. Beside the long, narrow flight of stairs leading to Charlie's quarters upstairs was a high, dark-brown wood-topped counter which all but hid the door under the stairs giving access to the back room. Well into the evening a small-boned unassuming man with a wispy white queue, wearing steel-rimmed spectacles and black cotton coat and pants, could be seen seated under the single naked light bulb dangling by a long wire from the high ceiling. At his back was a solid woodfaced wall of small drawers containing herbs and dried items, better unidentified, from which he supposedly selected remedies for the ailments of a sizeable clientele who were actually patronizing the gaming tables. No whites were allowed at the two ten-foot-long oval tables where twelve to fifteen or more Chinese would gather to play fan-tan. Chain smoking cigarettes or cigars, they would shuffle up to the table, make their bets on how many white markers would be left under the small cup when the dealer had finished removing them four at a time, then win or lose, walk away. Nothing was said, and there was never a change of expression on the faces of the participants, so watching a fan-tan game was about as entertaining as watching a funeral.

The gambling crowd, and many of the old Chinese, wanted no part of us and were downright sullen in our presence. Their attitude was in marked contrast to that of a group of relatively new Chinese brought out of Mexico by our forces when troops under the command of John J. Pershing stopped chasing Villa and his men and crossed back into the United States. They had operated food and liquor stands for our soldiers, and to keep them from being persecuted by Mexicans for having associated with Americans, the returning Army crossed them into the United States. Shortly thereafter, their residence in this country was legalized by a special act of Congress. They were so glad to be here, and to have been made legal residents by our government, they were extremely friendly to all Anglos and by preference had little or nothing to do with the old resident Chinese. They really had little in common with them, for they were more enterprising and up-to-date than the old timers. A large number of them opened grocery stores, and they ended up owning or managing practically all the restaurants in town. To my knowledge, the new Chinese were never mixed up with the gambling in Chinatown either, and they would have nothing to do with the opium imported by Chinese almost exclusively for the use of the older Chinese men.

There were several opium dens in El Paso, and they were frequented by a few Americans, most of whom were prostitutes from the adjoining red-light district, but opium was not one of the major problems faced by law-enforcement officers. Just as many individuals derive satisfaction from the feel, aroma, and smoke of a good cigar, the old Chinese were accustomed to smoking a few pipes of opium every day, seeking escape from a life that was bleak and a future that was almost hopeless. We were never able to connect Charlie Sam with opium, but the Service was well aware that he was the brains behind the smuggling of Chinese and tried several schemes to get him. Finally they brought in an inspector from another district by the name of Jim Kealy, a tall, lanky man with a great sense of humor who had been a cowpuncher in New Mexico and did not know the meaning of fear. Kealy hung around Chinatown; soon he became acquainted with Charlie Sam, and reportedly smoked opium a couple of times in one of the Chinatown dens to get in with the Chinese. Little by little, he gained Charlie's confidence. Then he casually inquired if Charlie knew of some way he could make a little money, for he was nearly broke. Charlie was leery, but after several weeks said he had a Chinese boy ready to enter the United States and for a price perhaps Jim would be willing to arrange for a drawing room on the El Paso Southwestern night train leaving for Kansas City. Jim bought the ticket, reserved the drawing room, and arranged for a Mexican taxi driver to take him and the boy to Newman, twenty miles north of town. There the boy was to be smuggled aboard the train on the blind side during the stop for water following the pull up the steep grade out of El Paso.

Kealy kept the office posted on all his maneuvers, coming in for one meeting with Inspector-in-Charge McKee, but most of the time reporting by telephone from various places in the city. His progress and plans were discussed in detail, particularly the idea of taking the boy off the train at Alamogordo in order to return him to El Paso for Charlie Sam's arrest and trial. Two of us voiced strenuous objections to the arrangements, the set-up not ringing true to us, but the plan went ahead as scheduled. No sooner was the boy installed in jail than a lawyer showed up. He produced papers to prove the boy was an American citizen; therefore, Charlie had committed no crime in arranging to send him north on the train.

Several years later I ran into Charlie Sam in Chinatown one afternoon. After we had shaken hands and he had offered me the usual cigar, he told me he was planning to return to China for the remaining years of his life. In honor of the occasion he invited me to his rooms, where he set out a jug of excellent heavy-bodied nut-flavored rice whiskey and two fragile porcelain cups. Over a couple of drinks he smilingly confided, "You didn't know it, but you almost caught me once with that Jim Kealy. I was a little suspicious of him, but thought I would try him out so I sent a native with him. If that boy had gone through, I planned to send two more; if they got through without any problems, I would have given him plenty of Chinese to smuggle in." We then talked over many things that had happened along the border in the years of our acquaintance. A lot of my hunches and suspicions received confirmation long after there was any point in taking corrective measures, and we parted with many good wishes for our unknown futures. Some weeks later a mutual friend told me Charlie had left, and apparently he had, for I never heard of him again.

VI

BORDER PROBLEMS

★ IN AN EFFORT to reduce the numbers of incoming aliens, and at the same time increase the percentage of those with some degree of education, Congress in February, 1917, passed the Literacy Act, requiring that every immigrant, barring a few specified exceptions, be able to read and write in some language. With a growing demand for laborers in this country and a deteriorating economic situation below the border, the Act promptly presented the Immigration Service with a major problem insofar as Mexicans were concerned.

For years peons had entered the country in the springtime to work on ranches near the line and as section hands or track layers for the railroads. As they applied and were admitted, they would be taken to the basement of the Immigration Service building and held until detailed individual examinations were completed. When a group could be released, guards would escort the men outside to the rear of the building and line them up. There agents representing the railroads and ranches would make speeches about the delightful quarters, good pay and fine food they would have if they went to work for their company. When the promising was over, the agents would shout, "This way for the Santa Fe," "This way for the Southern Pacific," and so on, the men following the agent they thought offered the best or the most benefits.

Few temporary workers were interested in staying here beyond their six-months work permit, for they were not used to our cold weather, and most had families in Mexico. As a result, when transportation back to El Paso was provided in the fall so they could return to their homes below the border, they usually went. According to Service records, one man came in on a work permit for ten years running and returned each winter to his family. With the passing of the Literacy Act, however, the great majority of these people became ineligible for legal admission and many started smuggling in. So long as work was available, they kept coming, and the proportionately few federal officers available to enforce the laws could not begin to make a dent in their numbers, no matter where or how they were detailed to patrol the line. Once north of it, the aliens remained away from the border if they could manage to do so, staying in larger cities such as Dallas, Fort Worth, Albuquerque, Phoenix and Los Angeles where there were sizeable groups of Mexican-speaking people instead of moving south as the temperatures dropped. To the extent that it was more difficult for all immigrants to get into the country, those who were admitted legally also were more apt to remain.

Residents near the border paid little or no attention to the comings and goings of Mexicans. They were accustomed to seeing them, knew they came in numbers during warm weather to work the crops, and accepted as an integral part of the economy the inexhaustible supply of cheap labor they represented. Because the Literacy Act directly affected the availability of laborers, and therefore the cost of their produce, many reputable farmers and ranchers facing sizeable increases in work-crew expenses continued to hire peons, regardless of the fact that they were in the country illegally. Some actually went so far as to impede the efforts of Immigration officers attempting to enforce the regulations. Thus the first hint of destructive disrespect for federal regulations and for the men charged with carrying them out, which spread so rapidly during Prohibition, began to influence the lives of people residing along the Mexico-U.S. border.

Immigration officers in the outside force and men in the Customs patrol had too much territory to cover to be able to stop all smuggling across the border, so they were usually assigned where they could do the most good. One Immigration Service detail watching the railroad tracks in the sandy country near Deming, New Mexico, apprehended so many aliens that the Southern Pacific had to put on two special coaches to carry them back into Mexico. Many aliens apprehended as they left border communities for inland areas were rounded up and given "voluntary" returns to Mexico at the nearest port of entry unless there was some legal reason to hold them for prosecution.

The impoverished Mexicans, whose only interest was to earn

money that would enable them to live better and improve the conditions under which their families existed, had no desire to fight and seldom put up much of an argument when caught. We might pull a gun as a precautionary measure when approaching a group of them hiding out under a bridge, or when examining a cleaver-wielding Chinese cook in a restaurant, but after our initial challenge to surrender was made, we seldom had any problems. Even the guides were more apt to desert their charges and disappear back across the Rio Grande than risk being caught by staying with them, for they were mostly small-time operators interested in making what money they could without becoming entangled with the law. With so much country to cover, our greatest advantage lay in the fact that over a period of time the smugglers tended to follow a pattern. They crossed in the same way, at the same general spot, near landmarks they could locate readily in the dark, and so could we.

One stretch of the river where numerous aliens crossed was just west of downtown El Paso, directly opposite the Union Depot. Shortly after everyone in the office had gone to lunch, leaving me on duty with one of the male stenographers for company, a switchman telephoned in to report that two of our outside officers were pinned down behind the depot by rifle fire from across the river. With no alternative but to lock the office, I grabbed a Springfield rifle and two or three boxes of ammunition from the supply room, and with the stenographer to drive, set out in the only transportation available: the truck we used for a patrol wagon. When we reached the depot and parked the truck, I crawled to within shouting distance of the two officers. So long as they stayed put, they were fairly safe near the water in a large hole at the base of an uprooted tree. Raising up cautiously, I could see there was no shelter for them if they left the hole, and at the same time I spotted the rocks protecting the Mexicans firing at them. Realizing that the only way to put a stop to the shooting was to get at the Mexicans from an angle, I told the officers not to move and I crawled back across the tracks. Running along in a semi-crouch to stay behind the railroad embankment, I worked my way up river around the bend to a point where the men doing the shooting were exposed. Taking deliberate aim because of the distance, I pumped out three or four shots in rapid succession. At the second or third, one of them jumped from cover as if he had been stung and took off south on the run. I threw a few more shots after him for good measure, which increased his speed somewhat but also gave the others a chance to get away.

Weeks later, a Mexican strolled into the office and told the clerk at the front desk he wanted to see Señor Perkins. After being ushered to the door of the office where I was working, he ambled through, looked me over deliberately, then greeted me with a smiling, "Hallo, Perkeens. You know you shoot me?" Puzzled by his knowing my name and acting as though there was something humorous about a shooting, I asked him "When? And where?" Laughing, and telling me I was some fine shot, he said he had been one of the men shooting from the rocks at the two officers in the hole on the river bank behind the depot. With the admission that one of my bullets had accounted for his speedy departure from the scene, he dropped his pants. On each buttock were two tiny round scars from a bullet passing through about an inch below the surface.

Beyond the depot toward the smelter district was another spot often used by smugglers that was especially dangerous for us to cover. At that point the river channel through the caliche, or pale sand-colored clay, was rather narrow and the water came to within about a hundred yards of the road paralleling the main rail line out of the city. The north bank of the river rose rather abruptly to the road and then again to the railroad tracks, whereas the south bank was low and almost flat. Duty on the river was so dirty and our olive drab uniforms were so conspicuous that we always wore old clothes, but even in nondescript attire we were sitting ducks to smugglers against those caliche banks, especially on nights when the moon was shining.

One night when a group of aliens starting across the river was challenged by a couple of officers staked out near the water, the guides responded with rifle fire. Because so many shots were being fired so steadily, one of the officers scrambled back across the tracks to the depot and phoned for reinforcements. (We heard later that several *federales* had heard the shooting and joined in for the fun of it.) Three other off-duty officers and I were ordered in to the office as fast as we could be reached, putting an abrupt end to one of Gladys' and my rare Saturday evenings out. Dropping her at the house, I stopped for one man who lived near me, drove to the office so we could pick up rifles and ammunition, and then headed out the smelter road. By the time we reached our men on the river, they were running low on ammunition, and it quickly became obvious to me we had not brought enough to hold our own in the barrage until we could get them out of danger. Hurrying back to the depot, I put in a telephone call to the company of soldiers stationed at the smelter because of uprisings along the border. When I was put through to the officer in charge of the detachment, a Lieutenant Charles Stevens, I was surprised and delighted to discover we knew each other, having become acquainted while we were in Douglas. With a hurried agreement to get together, I outlined our situation and he promised to send us a supply of ammunition right away.

By and large, the Military always cooperated with us and with the other Services, so I told Lieutenant Stevens we could also use some assistance. He surprised me, under the circumstances, by replying that he could not give me any help without an official request from me, but with that bit of formal red tape quickly disposed of, he promised support was as good as on its way. Several hours later, one of the men in his company remarked that in camp Stevens had told his first sergeant he wanted about twenty volunteers to accompany him to the river where the Immigration Service was involved in a little gun play. By the time the word had been passed and the detail was ready to leave, there were considerably more than twenty soldiers who had grabbed rifles and were ready to join the fight. Those extra men turned out to be especially welcome, for practically every automobile on the road from town to the smelter district had stopped, a good-sized crowd had gathered to see what was going on, and the whole situation had become extremely ticklish. Stationing a half-dozen soldiers on the road to keep traffic moving, Lieutenant Stevens and I assigned most of the reinforcements to strategic spots along the river. His best marksmen were sent upstream around the bend, with orders to station themselves among the rocky outcroppings and pick off the smugglers from that angle.

While the shooting was at its height, one of the soldiers near me suddenly commenced yelling, "Lieutenant! Lieutenant! I'm shot! I'm bleeding. I'm going to bleed to death! Help, somebody, anybody! Help!" Without stopping to think about how clearly my dark clothes stood out against the caliche, I abandoned the rock behind which I had been lying and raced to the injured man, who proved to be a husky fellow weighing something over two hundred pounds. While Lieutenant Stevens and I were carrying our casualty to the back side of the railroad embankment where we could examine him, Stevens' uniform apparently presented a poorer target than my suit, for the Mexicans seemed to concentrate their fire at me, their bullets coming so close I could feel bits of gravel ricocheting against my legs. My concern for the man we were carrying prevented me from worrying about my own exposure at the time, but it was not long before I was irritated enough to face bullets again just to get that soldier back into the fight. On checking, we found he was barely creased through the skin at the base of his neck and was a long way from being in any danger of dying. Although blood was oozing through his shirt, he could easily have walked all the way to Fort Bliss on the other side of town and back.

The next day Lieutenant Stevens called to ask if I would go to Fort Bliss with him the following morning as his commanding officer wanted to talk to us about the report he had turned in on the fight. When we met in the Colonel's office, he told us he was always glad to have the Army assist the Immigration Service in the enforcement of laws, but this affair meant he had to account for several thousand rounds of ammunition, and he needed more details to do so properly. When I finished relating what had happened, corroborating Stevens' report, the Colonel leaned back in his chair. Squinting through the smoke of his cigar, he said, "I know both of you men did what you considered was right, but I think your tactics were wrong. In a situation like this, you should have withheld your fire and remained quiet. When the men shooting at you moved closer, you would have had better targets and could have done some real damage with much less ammunition." Without once raising his voice, the Colonel left us with the distinct impression that we had a lot to learn before we would measure up to his idea of officers in proper command of a situation. No disciplinary action was taken against either of us, and the soldiers probably enjoyed the unexpected action. But it was a long time before that lesson in tactics was sufficiently part of my mental processes for me to put the memory of the teacher behind me.

Within a week we heard that while our only casualty was the soldier with the neck wound, three Mexicans had been hit, and two of them had died. We were not always so fortunate, however. Close to the railroad spur west of the Santa Fe Street Bridge was a maze of crude shanties and cheap apartment houses. The apartments were shabby two-and-three-room units and usually had no facilities other than cold running water, a few electric lights, and a couple of toilets on the ground floor for use by all the tenants.

We had been shot at from the shacks and apartments on several occasions, and one of our men had been wounded, so when we received a tip that aliens would be crossing the river at that point, we decided to try to put a stop to people firing at our backs from the shelter of the buildings. After dark, I took Carpenter, who was one of our best shots, and two more men to the river. While two of us stationed ourselves behind one of the buildings, but facing the apartments instead of the river, the other two located themselves closer to the water to watch for the aliens. When the smuggler came across with four customers strung out behind him and had been challenged by the men near the river, two Mexicans with rifles hurried out of one of the apartment buildings and started firing towards our officers. From our position beside the building and to their rear, Carpenter and I opened fire and cut them down right where they stood, putting an end for quite some time to one problem in that vicinity.

Locating ourselves behind objects that provided adequate shelter close to town without being seen was always rather difficult, because on nights when smugglers intended to cross the river they usually arranged for spotters to be in the vicinity late in the afternoon. We always had to be on the alert for them, for mostly they were of Indian descent and extremely adept at deceiving people about what they were really doing. Singly and in pairs, they would stroll up and down along the water's edge or the railroad tracks on the American side. Sometimes there would be a spotter covering the Mexican side of the river as well. At dusk, girls acting like sweethearts sometimes joined the men, and then it was doubly difficult to elude their searching eyes, for the couples, wandering back and forth even more deliberately, would stop every so often to embrace and kiss, enabling the men to thoroughly scan the area.

The procedure authorized by Immigration laws and regulations for verifying the status of an alien adjudged inadmissible at a port of entry provides that he be held for a hearing before a Board of Special Inquiry (now an Inquiry Officer). My first real promotion insofar as authority was concerned took effect September 1, 1917, when I was designated to act as Chairman of the El Paso Board of Special Inquiry. Much of the cross-examination before the board, then composed of three inspectors, with a stenographer to record the proceedings, was conducted in the Spanish of the border. It was a far cry from Castilian, the best being spoken along the Sonora line, probably because that state had more schools. The most corrupt I ever heard was spoken in the vicinity of Laredo. Because it was not unusual when officers had Mexicans with them for the entire conversation to be carried on in Spanish, a working knowledge of it was practically a prerequisite to duty at the line. The few men accepted into the Service who did not speak the language were, as a consequence, required to attend regular classes in Border Spanish conducted by one of the Immigration officers at Service headquarters until they developed an acceptable proficiency. I became so accustomed to thinking and speaking in Spanish that many times when the family asked me something in English, I would respond, without realizing, in Spanish. When Board hearings had all but eliminated the backlog of incoming aliens applying for admission, I was given the additional duty of handling the preparation and filing of cases for the prosecution of alien smugglers apprehended more than once. With that responsibility, I also began to assist the district attorney in court with the questioning of witnesses. Handling prosecutions was entirely different from examining applicants for admission. When aliens were taken into custody by a man on the outside force, they would be brought into the office and held in the detention quarters. The apprehending officer would turn in a report of the circumstances surrounding their entry and capture, and if there was a suspected smuggler in the group and it was possible to identify him, the officer would do so.

Prosecution investigations involved interviewing each individual separately and endeavoring to obtain the full story of his entry, including whom he had paid to be crossed and how much. It was often difficult to get aliens to give evidence against their smugglers because of threats made about what would happen if they did. However, after learning they were actually the victims of a racket, they would usually cooperate. If the facts of the matter justified, the smuggler, with a couple of the aliens he had brought in, would be taken to the Office of the United States Commissioner and a complaint filed against him. The suspect would be permitted to enter a plea of guilty or not guilty; then in most cases he would be bound over to the grand jury for trial under a bond set in accordance with the circumstances of the case. The aliens would usually be remanded to the custody of the Immigration Service and held in default of an appearance bond either in the Service detention quarters or the county jail. When the grand jury convened, it was my duty to present the cases against the smugglers, the aliens being taken to court so they could appear as witnesses. During the trial which followed, I would sit behind the district attorney, or assistant district attorney, to suggest lines of questioning, because there was no way he could familiarize himself with each case when there were so many. If a smuggler was found guilty by the jury, he would be sent to either the county jail or the federal penitentiary, depending upon the gravity of the case, and the aliens would be formally deported to Mexico.

After about a year, cases for prosecution became so numerous I was relieved entirely of work with the Board and was able to devote all my time to handling prosecutions. That put me in close contact with officers in the outside force again, for they were the men who caught the people being taken to trial. It also made me the focal point of all smugglers with a grudge to settle, for to them I personified the government. During one year alone we had over a hundred convictions, a few resulting in jail sentences of six months or so, but most in penitentiary terms of one to three years, and in some instances, five. So many of the smugglers took their convictions as personal affronts for which I was the cause that I began to receive quite a few threats: telephone calls at home in the middle of the night, letters promising revenge when the writer had served his time, and every so often word that some fellow due to be released from jail was talking about bumping me off.

People seldom do the things they talk about at great length. The dangerous individuals are those who have it in for somebody and quietly set out to get him, but there is never any way to tell for sure when a threat will be carried out. For years I rode the streetcar to the office, boarding on Alamogordo and changing in the Plaza to a Mexico or Second Ward car, then walking the rest of the way. As more smugglers were released from jail or prison who let it be known they had scores to settle with me, I began to take an increasing number of precautionary measures, including driving our car to work when I had to come home after dark. Hueco Street was solidly residential, with garages opening onto an alley. On Montana Street, directly across the alley behind our house, was a police substation. From the back windows of the station, which stood fifteen or twenty feet back from the alley, the policemen could see our garage easily. It would have been easy, however, for somebody to bushwhack me at night while I put the car away, so I worked out an arrangement with the police to improve my odds. The moment they saw the lights of my car in the alley, one of them would walk out of the station and stand near the garage while I opened the door, turned on the light, and put the car away. In the house, I figured there was less likelihood of someone taking a pot shot at me, but nevertheless that was when I began sleeping with my .45 Colt automatic under my pillow. It was comforting to me to know it was there, but it also came close to causing a tragedy. One way or another, I was doing my best to keep Gladys from learning of the increasing number of threats on my life, especially after the first few months of her pregnancy, even though the threats were making me nervous and jumpy. What I did not consider was my reaction to being awakened from a sound sleep by an unfamiliar noise, and seeing a figure outlined against the window. Instinctively, my hand went for the gun. It was pointed, and my finger was tensing in its pull on the trigger when the silhouette shifted and I broke out in an icy sweat, for I had been within a hair's breath of shooting the mother of my unborn child.

The risk of sooner or later killing a loved one hangs over the head of every man in a job that requires the use of a gun. If he continuously allows himself to be conscious of that risk, he will not be able to do the job he has to do, but the knowledge stays there behind his surface awareness until he puts the gun away for good. Gladys never knew of the shakes that tore me apart after her breathing slowed in sleep, or if she did, she never mentioned it. But from then on I never kept a shell in the chamber of an automatic. I figured if my mind was functioning enough for me to work the mechanism, I would be alert enough to be sure of what was going on.

VII

DEATH IN UNIFORM

✷ OUR COUNTRY'S INVOLVEMENT in World War I changed many things insofar as law enforcement by federal officers on the Mexican Border was concerned. Passage of the Immigration or Passport Act in May 1918, in an effort to prevent the entry of enemy agents into the country, provided that any alien coming into the United States had to have a document issued by a competent authority stating the bearer's point of origin, nationality and identity. The Act also provided that it was an offense to enter the United States at a place other than a port of entry, forcing aliens smuggling in to become more devious and putting far greater demands on men in the outside force.

To help enforce the Passport Act, the Army assigned cavalry units to patrol duty along the Rio Grande, which amounted to four or five men riding out of a station at stated intervals for three or four hours, then riding back. Because they rode through less difficult stretches and could be evaded rather easily, additional men were needed in the outside force who were rugged enough to patrol hostile areas on flexible schedules so people trying to enter illegally would never know when or where they might be encountered. The Immigration Service had positions below the grade of inspector known variously as mounted guards, mounted watchmen, and mounted inspectors, for which the Civil Service requirements were not as stringent as for officers technically qualified for port of entry work.

With Passport Act enforcement appropriations, the Service was able to hire a considerable force of men without Civil Service examinations, so recruits were sought from among the local ranchers and cowhands. Kight, Rawls, Torres, Perry, and Truesdale were fairly rough characters, but they could take care of themselves and knew how to fight. Perry, who developed into one of our most dependable officers and was one of the best men I ever knew, was an extremely mild-mannered, polite and congenial individual who had been employed as a gunman by a large New Mexico cattle company. Charles Birchfield, another Passport employee, came from a prominent New Mexico family which owned a large ranch west of El Paso. He was a hard working, honest officer who became one of the administrative wheel horses upon whom I depended for many years. We nearly lost him, however, when he received his first gunshot wound during a shootout near the smelter district which cost the life of Charlie Gardner, one of our most valuable men. Charlie was a quiet, soft-spoken man in his early thirties when he entered the Immigration Service after losing his small cattle ranch in New Mexico following several dry years. He was small and of rather slight build, weighing in the neighborhood of 135 pounds, a man who did not drink or swear, but he had coped with his share of drunken cowpokes and rustlers and could hold his own in any man's league. If Charlie were crowded into a corner, he would shoot first, literally or figuratively, and ask questions later.

Once he and Birchfield were breaking in a new man, and as part of the man's training took him out toward the smelter district one cold winter morning to check traffic. In the vicinity of the smelter, which was roughly three miles west of El Paso, scores of Mexican adobe shacks were strung out between the Rio Grande and the road for maybe three-quarters of a mile. These were occupied by workers at the smelters and a large brick yard across the river in New Mexico, a foot bridge enabling the Mexicans to work in the brick yard and live in Texas.

The three officers had been on duty for several hours when a horse-drawn wagon pulled up, two Mexicans in serapes and big straw hats hunched over on the seat. Walking up to the driver, Gardner asked, "What do you fellows have in the wagon?" and leaned over the side to look under the seat. With that, the other Mexican reached down, picked up a gun from between his feet and shot at Gardner. At the same time the driver pulled a gun from under his serape and shot Birchfield, after which both men jumped off the wagon, ran into the maze of shacks and dashed across the foot bridge. On the New Mexico side of the river they crossed into Mexico. The new man was so petrified he stood near the wagon, his rifle by his side, while the Mexicans escaped, even though they were in full view and in range of his gun except for the few minutes they were among the houses between the road and the foot bridge. Needless to say, he was one recruit who failed to pass his probationary period, and although the shooting made headlines in the local newspapers, with the cooperation of everyone immediately concerned his part in it never became a matter of public information.

Charlie Gardner died the next day without regaining consciousness. His life was lost over five cases of tequila — all the wagon contained — worth perhaps sixty dollars in Mexico. Birchfield recovered quickly so we were not too concerned about tracking down the Mexican who shot him, but every man who knew Gardner did his level best for the next several months to locate his killer. A $500 reward was offered by Charlie's friends and associates for information leading to the arrest of the guilty man, and well over a month later it produced a tip which told us who he was and where he lived. Within an hour we had located the smeltertown shack that was supposedly his, picked up a woman who admitted to being his wife, and found a picture in the house she identified as that of her husband. Somehow the man succeeded in staying one jump ahead of us. On one occasion we received word he was working in a charcoal camp about twenty miles east of Ciudad Juarez, but it did no good. By the time we arranged for a Mexican to go to the camp and pick him up, he had disappeared. The *rurales* knew we were looking for him too, and finally Captain González, who was a friend of mine, offered to help catch him. The captain was one of the most trustworthy individuals I ever worked with, a crack shot and as quick as greased lighting. As we were driving along the dirt road east of Ciudad Juarez one day on a check of the charcoal camp, he spotted a covey of quail and had shot the head off one with his Luger before I could put my foot on the brake. A few miles farther on we came to a checking station where Mexican Customs officers inspected merchandise to be transported down river. When the inspecting officer walked up to the car, I recognized him as a man we had sent to the penitentiary several years earlier for smuggling aliens. He recognized me, too, and promptly turned ugly, but before he could say anything, Captain Gonzales had whipped out his gun, stuck it in the man's face, and told him to shut up. With that, we proceeded down the road to the camp, but after checking for several hours and finding no trace of our man, we headed back to town.

Several days later, a Mexican "coyote" or informer came in. He told us he had located the killer of Señor Gardner and identified the picture in our display almost immediately. He was known to have rustled cattle, stolen horses, and been involved in the smuggling of aliens and dope, so we were not overly inclined to believe or trust him. But he was so positive about his information, he agreed to kidnap the killer and bring him across the river at a spot we selected about twenty miles east of El Paso. On the off-chance he was telling the truth and could do what he said, another officer and I rode down river late the following evening. At the appointed place and time, we heard a horse enter the water on the Mexican side and slowly proceed across, apparently carrying extra weight. In a few minutes the informer rode up, a man trussed up with pieces of rope and leather straps lying head down across the saddle in front of him. Pulling him off the horse and taking a good look at him, we realized he probably was not the man we wanted, so we told the coyote he would have to come to the office the next day about the reward money. He did not like that idea one bit, asking, "Aren't you going to kill him now? We could throw him in the river," to which we replied we never had any intention of doing that; the man had to be taken in for further questioning. The informer was insistent that if we killed him then and there and threw his body in the water, it would be all over; we would have no more problems, and he could have the reward. When we still refused to go along with his ideas, he got back on his horse. With an extremely disgruntled *"Adios!"* he rode back across the river into Mexico.

We wanted to turn our prisoner over to the U.S. marshal in case he proved to be Charlie's killer, but since the man had actually been shanghaied across the river, we knew we would not have much of a case in court. While we figured out what to do, we blindfolded him, tied his hands and feet onto the lead horse, and rode back to town. At the office, we had another officer telephone the marshal and report in a disguised voice that if he would drive to a particular intersection in the outskirts of El Paso and park at a certain time on the north side of a specified street, he would see a man get out of a car and walk towards his automobile. That man, the marshal was told, could be the killer of Charlie Gardner. The marshal may have known to whom he was talking but since he could not be positive, there was no way he would be able to testify who had turned the prisoner over to him. When we saw his car stop in the proper place, we removed the blindfold from our Mexican, told him to get out and walk across the street to the other car, which he did, and was taken into custody. The next morning, the marshal called our office, saying he had picked up a man he understood was wanted by us, and asking how soon we could send an officer for him. With that, one of the inspectors took off for our erstwhile prisoner. After questioning the man, we were soon satisfied he was not the one; however, to be absolutely sure, we picked up the killer's wife and brought her to the office. From the way she acted, we knew without a doubt she was not married to him. About that point I was beginning to be slightly concerned about what would happen if the story got out about how our prisoner had been brought into the United States, so we inquired if he would like to stay after questioning him to be sure he could meet the regulations. When he replied that he would, and we had the necessary identifying documents, the Immigration Service arranged to have his presence in the country legalized. In the meantime, I telephoned a friend who operated his own company and hold him we had a Mexican in the office who needed a job and promised to work hard. For several months after the fellow was put on the payroll, I dropped by from time to time to check up on him and never received a single complaint. Periodically, from then on, I heard from the man, each time with indications that he was making excellent progress in his adopted country.

Early in March of the following year, we caught a Mexican smuggling liquor who told us during interrogation that he knew the man who had killed one of our officers on the road near the smelter. Because he had been caught crossing liquor before, he had to be tried in court, but when it developed during preparation of the case against him that he had a family, I went to the district attorney's office and asked if action could be suspended providing the bootlegger agreed to help us catch the killer we were after. The men in the office always cooperated fully with us if it was possible to do so, and with their agreement, we released him. A few weeks later he called me at home one night to tell me the man we wanted would cross the river at a certain place, approximately when he would be moving, and that there would be two gunmen with him. Our informer also said he had to accompany the men, so I told him to drop to the ground the minute we challenged the group to surrender. Well ahead of the appointed hour, several officers were in position at one side of the trail they were expected to use. When four men came across and were ordered to surrender, sure enough, one fell to his knees immediately. Before the challenge could be completed, the man in the middle of the three still on their feet opened fire and was dropped like a stone by one of our officers. The dead man turned out to be the Mexican who wounded Charlie Birchfield instead of Charlie Gardner's killer, who was never caught.

Most of the time we were able to pick up the men we wanted in relatively short order, mainly because so many people find it difficult to quit when they are ahead. East of the Stanton Street Bridge, between the Pearson Mills and the packing house, there was an open area containing a jumble of heavy timbers and stacked lumber belonging to the sawmill. An hour or so after dark, three officers hiding in the timbers challenged a man who had waded the river carrying a rifle and two gunnysacks filled with liquor. Putting down the sacks with care, and while he was still in a crouch, the smuggler fired on the officers, one high calibre bullet striking Frank Clark below the heart and killing him instantly. In their efforts to help Frank, the officers forgot about his assailant, who escaped in the darkness. Men were detailed to hide in the lumber piles the remainder of the night as soon as the shooting was reported to the office, and just at daylight they saw a Mexican woman walk up to one of the lumber piles. Without hesitation, she leaned over and picked up an old single shot .45-.70 rifle, then turned and started back toward the shanties beyond the mills. The officers who followed her to her house found a young man who turned out to be the son of the woman who had the rifle, so both were brought to the office for interrogation. After lengthy questioning of first one, then the other, the son finally confessed to having shot Frank. With another case marked "Closed," the men in the outside force were able to resume their regular duties, and their families no doubt soon forgot to wonder about the extra hours they had put in, or that for a time they had appeared more upset than usual about something they would not discuss.

Forgetting about Charlie Gardner and Frank Clark was something else entirely, for informing a woman that her husband, and the father of her children, has been killed in the line of duty is one of the hardest things I ever had to do. Every wife of an outside law-enforcement officer lives with the knowledge that her husband is in a hazardous line of work. Nevertheless, in order for him to do his job to the best of his ability, she must face it, accept it, and put it out of her conscious mind so her concern for him will not show and influence his actions. Even so, accepting the unacceptable is no easier for her than for anyone else, and the agony of bearing such a message is impossible to forget. I recall, too, that after hearing about Frank, I had one of the men go out and buy me a box of twenty-five cigars, all of which I had smoked before we wrapped up the case and I left the office the following afternoon.

Three smugglers with burros cross river, unaware of waiting patrolmen.
[SMITHERS COLLECTION, HUMANITIES RESEARCH CENTER
THE UNIVERSITY OF TEXAS AT AUSTIN]

VIII

UP THE LADDER

★ THE YEARS during and immediately following World War I brought changes in my personal life. I joined the Home Guard after being turned down for a commission in the Army, as were all men who occupied what were termed "key government" positions. Mostly, the Home Guard spent time learning to march in formation and handle a rifle, but on several occasions we were called out to patrol the border, which was right down my alley, but I was dissatisfied through it all.

There are periods in life when a person seems to be going nowhere, and this was one of mine. It seemed there was always some congressman or senator willing to assure promotion for men appointed to the Service through political influence, but I did not know anyone with influence. My salary increases were few and small, adequate appropriations being difficult to obtain under a Department of Labor that was not much in favor. Some of my slow progress was my own fault. I had a quick temper, in spite of admonishings by Mr. Berkshire and Mr. McKee, and any time somebody made a pass at me, or a less-than-sober Mexican cussed me out for taking his liquor away when I was working on the bridge, I was perfectly willing to let him have it. What I could not see was that advancement comes with experience, and experience changes a man if he is willing to profit by it. I was learning to size up people, to control myself, and to complete job assignments in an acceptable manner, but it would be years before I found that a cigar was a satisfactory substitute for Mr. Berkshire's chewing tobacco in giving me time to think before I took action.

Tragedy was added to frustration in the death of my wife, the mother of my two small children. Gladys had a congenital heart condition and slipped quietly to the floor from her partner's arms during a dance on a rare evening out at the country club. The children's grandmother came to El Paso for several months to help me, but she could not satisfy their need for the only parent they had. Their need for me kept me going. Nevertheless, my off-duty hours dragged endlessly, causing me to run undue risks and to take my misery out more often than I like to remember on people caught breaking the law, and to drink too much.

The first indication that I was getting somewhere officially was my promotion in October, 1920, to the rank of Inspector-in-Charge of the twelve-man Chinese Division. This occurred following the death of Archibald McKee. It was a logical advancement, since I had been running the division when McKee was out of town, but it was especially gratifying because I had been dissatisfied with my situation for so long, and it helped me to pull myself together in short order.

I knew the men well and with their help had made a lot of good cases against alien smugglers, but even when I was in charge I found much in the situation that was hard to accept and difficult to correct. The division was not overloaded with talent and we were seriously undermanned. During World War I the Passport officers had proved themselves of considerable value, particularly in deterring cattle and horse thieves from running livestock across the border into Mexico. When peace was declared, however, their salaries stopped and most of them had to be released. In El Paso, ten or twelve of the best men were kept by adding them to the regular Service payroll. That quickly put a strain on allocated funds, yet even when local residents began bringing pressure to bear on their representatives in Washington because depredations had been resumed against their stock, Congress continued to balk at appropriating sufficient money to staff the outside force adequately.

The organization was a much better one when I took over than it had been before the war, and included four or five skilled investigators, but we continued to have two problems besides funds which seemed equally insurmountable: priorities and qualifications. Any force which merely augmented the authorized Immigration Service regular force carried out its responsibilities only after all port of entry assignments were made. During any so-called emergency or whenever an Immigrant Inspector was on vacation or sick, our officers were required to fill in; this would have been fine if the arrangement had also worked in reverse, but it did not. A man might be able to check traffic and get along with the public, but that did not mean he would be worth anything when it came to detecting smugglers.

Cultivating reliable sources of information was one of the biggest jobs we had; much of my time was devoted to visiting with the night watchman at the El Paso Milling Company on the river east of the Stanton Street Bridge and with the watchman at the slaughterhouse on the line. They were on duty all night, and often they saw things or picked up useful bits of information from friends who came to sit with them and shoot the breeze. We also received help from friends in the police department. If they nailed, say, a Mexican taxi driver-chauffeur for something that was not too serious, they would turn him over to me before he was released. By approaching him with the suggestion that he might be able to get out of his predicament by "kicking in with information," it was often possible to develop valuable leads. Taxi drivers were mixed up in a lot of crime, especially running dope, and because they tended to be a bunch of coyotes, no one involved with law enforcement had any scruples about putting legitimate pressure on them if it served a good purpose in the long run.

During the early twenties, we conceived some simple but fairly successful ways to stir up dissension among several gangs of smugglers operating in the vicinity of El Paso in order to disrupt their activities as much as possible with the few officers we had. The gangs operated independently and were poorly organized; even without sufficient evidence to pick them up, we reached the point where we knew most of the members by sight. A favorite stunt was for two of us to walk into one of the saloons frequented by gang members during the afternoons. Whenever we spotted a well-known smuggler, we would invite him to step down to one end of the bar so we could buy him a drink, knowing he would not want to appear antagonistic by refusing. Somewhat apart from the rest of the saloon's customers, we would casually ask him several innocuous questions in a low voice, all worded so he would have to respond with a "*Si, señor*" or affirmative nod, and possibly a friendly smile. Asking if his wife was well, if his son was in good health, and if the rest of his children were growing rapidly were standard parts of our routine. After the man had agreed with us several times, noticeably, we would smile, pat him on the shoulder, and effusively wish him well, then leave the establishment without speaking or looking at anyone else. It would not be long before word began to circulate that Emilio, or José, was becoming chummy with the Immigration officers and maybe was working for us.

Similar procedures worked equally well in the office. If we knew something specific about what a suspect picked up for questioning had been doing the previous week, such as crossing seven aliens, including some Italians, and taking them by car to a particular building for transportation on to, say, Chicago, we gave him the impression the information had been reported to us by a rival gang member. Also, knowing the smugglers were reluctant to refuse seemingly routine requests from us (because to do so might indicate they were up to something illegal) we developed the habit of requesting two known smugglers to come to the office ten to fifteen minutes apart, and making sure their paths crossed. An appointment would be set up with one at perhaps three o'clock, and the other at 3:15 or shortly before. When the second smuggler arrived, he would be detained on some pretext in the hallway leading to my office. Inside, by a prearranged signal such as a telephone call, I would terminate a friendly conversation with the first smuggler on a handshake, escort him out the door, and as we walked down the hall toward his waiting competitor I would clap him on the back, thank him for coming in, and tell him we were always glad to see him. Because of such methods, the smugglers reached the point where they were actually coming to the office and turning each other in, although we found it paid off to take the information they gave us with a grain of salt. If one smuggler reported another was bringing aliens across five miles east of El Paso, it proved advisable to check five miles west of the city. Put together and analyzed, however, reports from informers enabled us to keep track of which gangs were operating where, so that whenever word was received about a crossing planned at a certain point we had a fairly good idea who was involved, and how the job would be worked.

A rewarding climax to our efforts occurred one day when a Mexican came in and told us the boss he had been working with for some time was crossing aliens via the Island that night, how many he would have, and where they were to be delivered. Early that same afternoon the man scheduled to meet the party on this side showed up with the almost identical details. Capping things off, the chaffeur followed him an hour or so later to say he had been asked to pick up a group of aliens at a certain point along the river that night. To prevent our three informers from comparing notes later on and realizing they had turned each other in, we decided the deal had to be queered, so we planned to scare them off by a few strategically placed gunshots. The informers would expect us to show and they were aware we never worked alone; therefore, to carry out the plan with enough realism to be convincing, I selected the most impressionable and slowest thinking officer in the force to make the supposed apprehension. As we worked our way in and settled into a good hiding place where we could observe the trail to be used, I purposely pumped my cohort full of the wildest kind of ideas about how tough these birds were, that they would shoot without hesitation, and how alert and fast we would have to be to catch them. By the time the smuggler and his aliens showed up, my partner was almost rigid in fearful anticipation of the danger. Nor did a shout in his ear of, "That fellow's got a gun!" as I pulled my Colt .45 and put a bullet in the trail some distance from the leader stir him into any frenzy of action. While I fired a few more shots into the suddenly empty trail, he succeeded in pulling his gun, but before he reached a decision regarding his next move, we heard an automobile start up and leave, plus snapping twigs and rustling underbrush from the aliens' beating a hasty retreat. The ruse had worked! Not only that, it had worked so successfully two of the same informers returned later with more information.

For a change of pace, but mainly to know the men better, and because it was never easy to stay behind when they were facing gunfights at least a couple of times a week, I continued to go out occasionally with the patrols working the river. But increasingly my activities were connected with the results of, rather than involvement in, what the men were doing. For example, Strauss, New Mexico, was a rather important stop on the railroad where we stationed a horseback detail to catch aliens following the tracks through the sandy country after they crossed the river west of the city. With the discovery by officers in the detail that aliens were leaving the tracks to give the station a wide berth, the officers assumed their presence was known and commenced patrolling the rails beyond a bend east of Strauss. When a group of aliens walking the tracks in the middle of a cold winter night was challenged by Charlie Birchfield and another officer, their leader fired, hitting Charlie in the hip. The other officer returned the shot and dropped the guide in his tracks, upon which the aliens immediately surrendered. Marching them to Strauss, he put them under guard while Paul Jordan, who was in charge of the Strauss detail, went out to bring in Charlie.

A report of the event was relayed to me by the railroad telegrapher, and within an hour, relief officers were on their way to the scene. Because a man had been killed, I drove out via La Union in order to notify the Justice of the Peace there to impanel a coroner's jury for a trial. They followed me to Strauss in a large touring car, and following their arrival at the scene an inquest was held over a corpse that had already begun to freeze. Although I had been home in bed at the time of the shooting, my testimony, which merely related what the officers had reported, was all the evidence heard. While I was talking, the coroner went through the dead guide's pockets. Finding a few pesos, which he promptly adjudged a fine, and allowing a few seconds for deliberation, he returned a verdict through chattering teeth that, "Thees man, he come to die by freeze to death." With that, the corpse was fastened onto the running board of the touring car with bailing wire, head forward, and the thoroughly chilled jury, witnesses and onlookers returned to their respective communities to take up the business of another day.

Aliens did not always lose out, however. Two officers in the Strauss detail apprehended two aliens one night during particularly cold weather. Like most Mexicans trying to smuggle into the United

States, they were from the interior, and their thin cotton shirts and pants afforded no protection against our more rigorous climate. They were so obviously suffering from the close-to-freezing temperature, the officers took them down into a culvert and built a fire so they could warm up before starting the mile-long walk to Strauss. When their small fire burned down, one of the aliens was sent out to gather more wood, which he did, but he returned with a rock in one hand. Knocking out one officer while the other's attention was diverted, the two aliens jumped the second officer, knocked him out, and fled. Again, the station telegraph operator sent word through to us. Following receipt of the message from Strauss, three of us drove out with two horses in a truck to pick up the aliens' trail. With no means of transmitting information to men on scouting details about what was happening, patrols working in uninhabited country beyond crossroads or railroad stops were completely on their own. As a consequence, outside officers had to use their own judgment and ingenuity when tracking illegal entrants. We followed this pair for over twenty-five miles into Mexico, and well below Ciudad Juarez, before we saw the buildings of the city and thought better of continuing our pursuit.

Another afternoon about one o'clock, we came upon some tracks which we followed until we lost them in the darkness. By then we were well back from the river and lost, but our horses had been borrowed from a nearby ranch, so we gave them their heads to let them take us home. After a kick in the ribs, they started off down the slope of what was almost a mountain into country that was extremely rocky and arid. Because we had had nothing to eat all day and no water since morning, we were eager to reach a large tank we spotted in the distance about sundown. To our concern, when we reached the hole we found it was not only dried to a puddle of water about fifty feet across, but it was stagnant. Also, a dead cow was mired in the soft ground and partially immersed in the water. Our horses were as thirsty as we were, but they did not drink much, and we could not drink at all, though we did wet our hands and the backs of our necks, and the horses were revived enough to carry us the balance of the way to their home ranch.

The casual smuggling of Mexicans, involving one hiring another who knew the border country to act as guide for a few dollars, with no responsibilities beyond the river crossing, was entirely different from the smuggling of European aliens which increased the pressure on officers at the line almost immediately following passage of the first Quota Law in 1921. With that law, a limit was placed on the number of immigrants from each European country to three percent of the persons of that nationality living in the United States at the time of the 1910 census, and it particularly affected individuals from the countries of southern Europe. Formerly able to enter the country legally through such ports as New York, Boston and Philadelphia, European aliens desirous of joining relatives or friends already established here willingly paid several hundred dollars to be smuggled in and taken to the interior, or at least to a large city well inside the border. Europeans who went to Mexico City with this idea in mind usually boarded one of the passenger trains moving north through Chihuahua to Ciudad Juarez. During the journey, they would be contacted by representatives of the smuggling gangs, who were put on board to make contacts with aliens and guide them to selected rooming establishments in Juarez. At the boarding houses, more definite arrangements would be worked out, including a fee which cost from several hundred to a thousand dollars, but in any event, was all the traffic would bear. If the alien had no money, or not enough in the eyes of the smuggler's agent, but did know somebody inside the United States, the head man would be notified accordingly. He would get in touch with his contacts north of the border and arrange for collection of the necessary funds from the alien's relative or friend.

Except for a group organized to bring Greeks into the country and deliver them by automobile to Denver via Raton, New Mexico, and a move to cross some Italians who were suspected of belonging to the Mafia, the smuggling of European aliens across the border was a relatively unplanned, informal operation. The leader of the gang seldom accompanied the aliens across the Rio Grande, arranging instead to have them brought over by coyotes, many of whom were drug addicts or were wanted on the American side for one reason or another. Once the guide was set and the time and destination worked out, the boss would come across to set up a primary destination for the party. That would be in some house near El Paso where the aliens could stay until they were moved on to a secondary destination, sometimes as far away as St. Louis. Transportation was usually provided by one of the Mexican-operated taxi companies, which were actually nothing more than several Mexicans who owned cars and operated them out of vacant lots. Taxi licenses would be secured for the cars, telephones installed, and somebody assigned to stick around to take calls, but each operator worked independently and did pretty much anything for money. At the time agreed upon, guides would take the aliens from the houses in Juárez to the appointed places on the river, turn them over to coyotes for crossing and delivery on this side to taxi drivers who would take the aliens to their first hideout.

The group smuggling Greeks into the country through Raton was well enough set up to elude us whenever we followed up on a tip and checked for them on the highways, so we worked out an alternate plan to pick them up in Raton, gambling that they would not be vigilant so far from the border. Within two hours of receiving a telephone call from an informer that some Greeks were set to be crossed, Inspector Kight, who was more or less my right-hand man, and I left for Raton. Our unmarked government Chevrolet touring car was not the best automobile available for such a trip, but it certainly was a tremendous improvement over the Model T's the Service acquired around 1914 to replace horses and buggies. Toward morning, we pulled off the road for a short nap, but the dirt highways north through Las Cruces and Albuquerque were fairly good and by frequently changing drivers, we covered the 450 miles to Raton in slightly over twenty-four hours.

A coded telegram was awaiting us at our hotel when we finally arrived late the following afternoon, indicating that five Greeks had left El Paso just before noon. Presumably, they were en route to Raton, which would put them right behind us. As soon as we cleaned up, we began checking around town, supposedly for a place to eat dinner, and learned two of the restaurants were run by Greeks.

Further inquiries eliminated one, and we settled down to watch the other, all night if need be. Shortly after 1:00 in the morning, an automobile pulled up in front of the building and seven men got out, two of whom later proved to be chauffeurs. Kight and I moved behind them through the front door and, after identifying ourselves, we took everyone in the restaurant into custody, including the proprietor. With the cooperation of the local authorities, we committed them to the care of the city jailer, charging the restaurant owner with active conspiracy in the smuggling.

When we had finished at the jail, we walked back to our hotel room, but after undressing and climbing into bed we found we were much too tired and keyed up to go to sleep. Kight and I lay there talking in the dark for ten or fifteen minutes, then gave up, deciding to take in the sights of Raton, reportedly a wide open "anything goes and usually does" town. Even at that late hour, Kight's sense of humor was functioning, for on the spur of the moment he suggested, "Let's put on our uniforms instead of the clothes we took off, and see if we can have some fun." Within ten minutes, complete with guns, we took off for Railroad Avenue, where most of the saloons, honkytonks and houses for gambling and prostitution were located. Expressionless, we strolled down the Avenue towards the gaudily decorated bright spots which offered twenty-four hour entertainment to the raucous, importuning accompaniment of tinny pianos and other assorted off-key, off-tune musical instruments. Raton residents were obviously unfamiliar with our uniforms, but they were not slow in reacting to two men wearing badges of some sort; they vanished like wraiths into thin air at our approach. A few feet inside the doors of the first saloon we entered, we stood for several minutes calmly surveying the house and apparently checking out every conscious occupant in view. Then we exchanged a glance, turned around, and walked out. Next door, we followed the same routine. By the time we were outside the third place, every remaining establishment on the Avenue was dark. Without saying a word, we had closed up the town! The next morning, with five or six hours' sleep, we left Raton; during the succeeding days we wore our uniforms on the business for which we had brought them: contacting peace officers. In Las Vegas, Santa Fe, Albuquerque, Socorro, Las Cruces, and nearly every small town we drove through, we stopped to solicit assistance in the apprehension of aliens, explaining what to look for in identifying individuals as aliens being transported across country by smugglers and how to contact us.

The Southwestern desert where alien tracks were followed.
[SMITHERS COLLECTION, HUMANITIES RESEARCH CENTER
THE UNIVERSITY OF TEXAS AT AUSTIN]

IX

PROHIBITION

✻ BY FAR THE GREATEST CHANGE in conditions along the border was the burden on law enforcement officers which resulted from passage of the War Act of November 21, 1918, and the Eighteenth Amendment to the Constitution, which declared all liquors with more than 0.5 percent alcohol to be intoxicating. To prevent their manufacture, sale and transportation, the Volstead, National Prohibition, or Prohibition Enforcement Act was passed over President Wilson's veto on January 17, 1920. Up to that point, federal officers had been highly respected by everyone, even more than state, county and city officers; criminals usually hesitated to shoot at them, except possibly in moonshine country and some of the southern states. However, with higher salaries available in private industry, it was all but impossible for the government to obtain enough qualified officers to enforce the Prohibition Act and, within a relatively short time, some federal officers were known to be taking bribes from liquor smugglers. Contributing equally to the change in public attitude was the rather understandable feeling on the part of many veterans who had fought with the Allied Expeditionary Forces in countries whose citizens drank wine instead of water, that Prohibition had been passed behind their backs. As such, it was a law which deserved neither their recognition nor support. With the growing disregard for the law and the increasing lack of respect for law enforcement officers, the attitude toward federal officers on the part of residents on both sides of the line deteriorated noticeably. Whereas alien smugglers as a rule had not been inclined to fight, liquor runners were. Most of them were criminals wanted for a variety of major offenses in both the United States and Mexico, and they would fight at the drop of a hat, with pistols or rifles. So gunfights came to the Rio Grande, and officers working along the border commenced carrying rifles as part of their regular equipment. So, too, there were increasing instances of officers' firing at each other while working the river at night, for there was no sure way to determine whether somebody approaching was a fellow officer, a Customs Service line rider, a Prohibition officer, or a smuggler bringing whiskey or aliens into the country.

In an effort to cut down the risks officers were running on the river of being shot by other officers, we began working in pairs, and cooperating with the Customs and Prohibition men to prevent coming into contact with each other. The officer in charge of the Customs patrolmen on the river would choose the territory they would cover one week, while the Immigration Service outside force covered the rest; the next week Inspector McKee would choose the section we were responsible for, and Customs took the rest. To avoid further complications, whenever the Immigration Service received a tip that liquor was to be brought over, which was in the province of Customs as an arm of the Treasury Department also having jurisdiction over Prohibition men, we would be withdrawn from the locale and their officers would be substituted. The same thing would happen whenever Customs learned aliens were to cross. In that way, if the case was blown, a Service not actually having jurisdiction would not be blamed.

Jealousy existed between outside men and the officers on the river, but it was kept to a minimum because Grover Webb, the head of the Customs Service in El Paso, was a very fair minded, efficient officer as well as an able supervisor. Neither of us would permit criticism of officers in the other Service, even though it might be justified, and each of us knew we could count on the other's cooperation in solving our mutual problems. The Customs Patrol, which developed from the Customs line riders, comprised about a dozen men in El Paso, plus others stationed outside of the city. Our work with them along the Mexican border was of an entirely cooperative nature, but after the Border Patrol was set up in 1924, it proved to be a larger and better organization, so the Customs Patrol was discontinued. (Later they did have a force on the Canadian border to prevent liquor smuggling.)

As illegal liquor outlets developed in the United States, and fairly dependable supply lines were established, Mexican wholesalers commenced guaranteeing delivery to points within a twenty mile zone inside the United States for an additional ten dollars a case. This insured the buyers not only against having their liquor confiscated by officers at the border, but also against having it stolen by the runners themselves for resale elsewhere. To guard the shipments while they were being smuggled into the country, and thereby insure themselves against unnecessary losses, the wholesalers began hiring the toughest men they could find, men who would not hesitate to run over any officer attempting to flag them down on the road. If they had a good load, they would shoot their way through. Criminals wanted on both sides of the line were hired because they would fight rather than be caught with their cargo, and also hired were narcotics addicts, who would fight anybody, anytime, on little more than a change of expression. Americans running liquor to points in the interior such as Albuquerque, Denver, La Junta and Kansas City, were well organized and used elaborate precautions in moving their merchandise. One of their favorite vehicles was the Buick roadster, and they often sent out four cars to take one or two loads through, an empty car being sent ahead to determine whether or not officers were working the highway. They used all sorts of signals, including flashing tail lights, to warn following cars, and they reacted quickly when we started passing up the head cars by sending the loaded ones first. Considering the risks, expenses, and the fact that the liquor cost about thirty-five dollars a case delivered to their cars near El Paso, the operation was not too lucrative even when retailed at around one hundred dollars a case in, say, Denver. With larger crews of guards used to cross liquor, duty on the river near El Paso became so dangerous that three, four, and sometimes six officers, instead of two, were assigned to work together, and they often carried shotguns as well as rifles. One or two men would take up positions behind large stumps or in a ditch where they would be safe, and the rest would find separate hiding spots. When smugglers showed up, one federal officer would call out instructions to halt, put up their hands, and surrender. Invariably, his answer would be a hail of bullets, but by then the other officers could tell where the smugglers were and return the fire. Their shots would draw the smugglers' bullets away from their initial target, giving the officer a chance to change his position sufficiently to enter the fight with some degree of security.

El Paso was by far the worst place on the border for gunfights, although one good thing could be said: the smugglers considered the whole thing a kind of game, and when they lost out, that was pretty much all there was to it. Around Brownsville, and in the lower Rio Grande Valley from Rio Grande City to Port Isabel, the smugglers took shootings very seriously, and several officers were killed by shotgun blasts in the face when they answered their doorbells at night. Gunfights on the job never worried me. The fact that at times I had to kill another human being was part of the duty and did not weigh on my conscience afterwards to any extent, because the only time I did shoot was to protect myself or someone else. When my life, or that of another officer, was in danger, it seemed to me the person killed was simply less fortunate than the survivors, and his bad luck should not disturb me later. Thinking can be a problem in other ways, however.

Since our contacts with smugglers increasingly produced bullets in response, it became difficult to hold our fire in questionable situations until we could be sure of what was going on. Indicative of the tension the men were under was an instance which occurred two or three hundred yards from the river below Cordova Island, where a large stand of tall reeds, riddled with narrow, crooked paths leading to the water, was a favorite crossing point for smugglers and required almost nightly surveillance. The dried-out reeds made such loud rustling noises because of occasional gusts of air, to say nothing of moving of animals and people, that it was difficult to work there and stay calm in the daytime, much less after dark. On a storm-black night when three of us were watching the trails from the outer edges of the reeds, one man's imagination produced an alien, with rifle, out of the rustles caused by something approaching. He challenged the sound with a hollered, "Halt, and throw up your hands." When the rustlings continued despite his second challenge of, "Halt and throw down your gun!" he shot at the sound, hitting a yearling heifer between the eyes. We all understood his jitters, but it was a lot easier for him to locate the owner of the calf by its brand, and pay him for it, than to live down his four-legged alien.

Possibly the most cold blooded killing of officers, particularly federal men, occurred at the Sherman Hog Ranch on the eastern outskirts of El Paso. The Shermans were suspected by El Paso law enforcement officers of being involved with big-time smugglers of contraband liquor, so we tried to steer clear of their property. On a tip, six or seven Prohibition officers went out to the ranch one night with a warrant to search the place and walked into a hornet's nest when they returned the shots that killed two members of their group during their approach to the main building.

It was late at night when my phone rang and the officer on duty told me Prohibition authorities had contacted Customs and Immigration for help with a fight at the Sherman Ranch. I instructed him to call ten of the best shots we had, and by the time a car picked me up and we reached the vicinity of the fighting, officers from various Services were gathered at the scene discussing strategy. Vegetation in the area was limited to small greasewood bushes from a few inches to perhaps a foot in height, and was so sparse that the wind-rippled sand resembled a white sea against which every one of us stood out sharply in the bright moonlight. To make matters worse, there was not a sign of a cloud in the sky or trace of haze to offer the slightest shadow while we worked our way to within rifle range of the house. Nevertheless, after consulting with the officers in charge from the other Services, we decided we should spread out and encircle the ranch. When everybody was in position, a signal to advance was passed from man to man and we started to close in. We soon reached the bodies of Beckett and Woods, but finding them past any need for attention, we continued to reduce our circle to the point where two or three officers were able to work their way up against the main house. With the building for protection, we called to the Shermans to come out with their hands raised. When no reply was forthcoming, one officer raised his hat into an open window on the barrel of his rifle. As that produced no response, another officer hiding in the shadows behind the house slipped inside through an open door, only to discover the occupants had fled, leaving nothing behind them but a bunch of empty cartridges.

It was never clearly established under exactly what conditions the killings had occurred, but from the positions of the men's bodies, and other evidence found at the scene, it appeared they had been fired upon from the house without warning and had died instantly. When the case against the Shermans came up on the court docket, their attorney succeeded in securing a change of venue to a small town in West Texas because of the strong feeling against them in El Paso. For weeks before their trial took place, the Shermans attended church where they were to be tried and contributed to the local charities. The verdict was for their acquittal.

Apprehension of smugglers was often swift and violent.
[SMITHERS COLLECTION, HUMANITIES RESEARCH CENTER
THE UNIVERSITY OF TEXAS AT AUSTIN]

X

BORDER PATROL

★ THE UNITED STATES BORDER PATROL as it is presently organized dates from June 1, 1924, when it officially took over duties that had been carried out by Immigration Service officers in the outside (Chinese) division. In the years immediately after, the Service was forced to terminate most of the Passport Act employees, one man spearheaded efforts in Washington, D.C., to have money appropriated for men who would be assigned strictly to patrol duties along the border. That person was Congressman Claude Hudspeth, who owned a large sheep ranch near Del Rio, on the Devils River, and was truly representative of stockmen along the upper Rio Grande. He headquartered in El Paso, where he was a resident most of the time when he was not in Washington, and where he was a frequent visitor to Immigration offices. Being intimately familiar with problems along the line, Congressman Hudspeth was well aware of the need for more men in the outside force and of the fact that they would be used as a supplement to the regular Immigration Service force until some form of patrol was established by law under a separate appropriation.

On May 28, 1924, Congress passed an act limiting immigration from almost all countries and authorized the appropriations necessary to enforce it. Through Congressman Hudspeth's efforts, a rider was attached to the appropriations bill which was effective July 1, 1924, providing that "at least one million dollars of this amount shall be expended for additional land border patrol, of which one hundred thousand dollars shall be immediately available." That was all the legislation the Border Patrol had as a basis for creating an additional branch of the Bureau of Immigration and Naturalization in the Department of Labor.

Early the following year, Congress passed another bill which provided one million dollars for a coast and land border patrol, and gave any employee of the Immigration and Naturalization Service the power without warrant: (1) to arrest any alien who in his presence or view is entering or attempting to enter the United States in violation of any law or regulation made in pursuance of law regulating the admission, exclusion, or expulsion of aliens, or any alien who is in the United States in violation of any such law or regulation and is likely to escape before a warrant can be obtained for his arrest ... (2) within a reasonable distance from any external boundary of the United States, to board and search for aliens any vessel within the territorial waters of the United States and any railway car, aircraft, conveyance or vehicle, and within a distance of twenty-five miles from any such external boundary to have access to private lands, but not dwellings, for the purpose of patrolling the border to prevent the illegal entry of aliens ... and (3) to make arrests for felonies which have been committed ... under any law ... regulating the admission, exclusion, or expulsion of aliens.

Before introducing his amendment, Congressman Hudspeth consulted with Immigration officials and interviewed officers at El Paso many times, especially District Director George J. Harris, so most of us were well aware of what he intended to do. District Director Harris was extremely enthusiastic about the proposed Patrol but his duties in connection with the administrative staff — as well as with Immigrant inspectors, accounting, and detention personnel under the assistant director and the Chinese Division under me — left him little time to devote to the details of its formation. Therefore, when word came through that funds had been made available for a Border Patrol, Mr. Harris called me to his office about another assignment, and for the next six months or more my principal job was to develop and implement a plan of action for the new organization.

At the outset, ideas were gathered from similar organizations, such as the Canadian Mounted Police, the Michigan State Police, and the Pennsylvania Constabulary. Every enforcement unit contacted was most cooperative, not only in providing details concerning their operations but in proffering suggestions and recommendations for our consideration. When the fundamentals were worked out, I called on two longtime associates and good friends from my Tucson days for their opinions and advice: John F. Harne and Walter Miller, both of whom had taken over as Inspectors-in-Charge of the outside forces at Marfa, Texas, and Tucson, Arizona, respectively. In the final planning stages, we were also fortunate to have the enthusiastic assistance of Walter E. Carr, the district director from Los Angeles. About eighteen months were required from the time the Border Patrol was authorized for primary regulations to be adopted in Washington, D.C., and it was three years before the Patrol was extended to cover Florida and the Canadian Border. Many changes have been made since then, and the Border Patrol is a much larger organization, but fundamentally it still operates along the lines of the general plan John Harne, Walter Miller and I put together.

When first established, the Border Patrol covered only the U.S.-Mexican border, and administrative areas conformed to the boundaries of the three Immigration Service Districts. The Los Angeles District covered from the border north to just beyond San Luis Obispo, California, and from the Pacific Coast to approximately fifty miles east of Yuma, Arizona. The El Paso District extended from there to Devils River, Texas. The San Antonio District ran from that point to Brownsville on the Gulf. Each district was divided into sectors, El Paso having three: from roughly Yuma, Arizona, to the Arizona-New Mexico state line with a head office originally in Nogales, and later Tucson; from the Arizona state line to just east of Sierra Blanca, Texas, with supervisory personnel stationed in El Paso; and from about Sierra Blanca to Devil's River, with headquarters at Marfa. Walter Miller, Johnny Harne and I became the first Patrol Inspectors-in-Charge in the El Paso District. All of us, interestingly enough, were "Burnett trained."

The initial Border Patrol uniform was forest green with blue cuffs and epaulets, a forest green shirt, and a black tie, taken primarily from the Canadian Mounted Police, with silver insignia for the men and gold for supervisory personnel. Pants were cut like riding breeches, and leather puttees, Army-issue shoes and Sam Browne belts completed the military appearance of the uniform. In cooler climates, caps were uniform, but in Texas we wore stiff-brimmed Stetsons with Cordovan-brown hat bands, more suitable for that part of the country; for summer wear, we adopted a lightweight olive green cotton shirt and trousers combination.

A man had to be over twenty years of age to apply for a position in the Border Patrol and be a citizen of, or owe permanent allegiance to, the United States. If accepted, he had to be twenty-one when he began duty and in excellent physical condition. A training program was set up for new men, during which they reported two or three times a week for lectures on investigative and inside procedures given by men in the Service and volunteers from the Police Department, sheriff's and district attorney's offices. In El Paso, the twenty-six men in the outside force were blanketed into the new organization while wheels were set in motion to bring the Patrol up to its authorized force as rapidly as possibly. In the hopes of being able to select new men from applicants who had passed Civil Service examinations for other government positions, we contacted the Civil Service Commission for lists of such individuals, but in the absence of such we received the names of men who had taken the examination for the Railway Mail Service. Several were interviewed but few qualified, since the character of our work was entirely different; therefore, additional employees were recruited on a temporary basis until suitable Civil Service examinations could be prepared and given.

Headquarters were set up in an abandoned barracks building and garage which had been used by the Military Police during the war. The first floor of the building was turned into a large assembly and report room, a store room, and offices for my assistant, Willis B. (Bud) Perry, a clerk, and myself. The upstairs was partitioned into permanent living quarters for several of the single men, and the balance was fixed up as a dormitory for use by off-duty officers. The garage became a repair shop for our four (and hopefully more) assigned government vehicles. Automobiles were not too reliable, even in town, but we managed to start out with three Model-T Fords and a converted Reo truck for a patrol wagon to haul prisoners captured on the river to detention facilities.

To obtain some publicity for the newly established Border Patrol, we arranged to have the men in the El Paso Sector entered as a unit in the 1924 Armistice Day parade, which was an important part of that holiday celebration. At Mr. Harris' direction, the Seventh Cavalry at Fort Bliss was requested to furnish us with horses, and all but two officers participated. The Patrolmen made an excellent appearance, as most of them were fine horsemen anyway, and we received widespread notice, photographs and write-ups appearing in Arizona, New Mexico, and California newspapers, as well as in Texas.

Because of the topography of the surrounding country, most of our work had to be accomplished on horseback, and thanks to the government practice of seldom doing things in the most practical way, I got myself into a slight jam over that. The men were supposed to receive thirty dollars a month to cover the cost of their horses, tack, and feed while on scouting details. (They used their own weapons and drew ammunition from the Army until arrangements could be made for the Service to issue regulation Army 30-06 rifles, Winchester .12 gauge sawed-off shotguns, and .38 calibre Colt revolvers.) The allowance for horses was reasonable, in view of the fact that a good half-broken horse cost from sixty to seventy-five dollars, and the pick of a couple of hundred mounts might run as high as one hundred fifty dollars, but horses could not be shifted readily from place to place, forcing me to use the man whose horse was in a given location rather than matching a man's talents to the job's requirements. To solve this situation, I called the men together and they agreed to turn their thirty dollars over to the office each month and let the office provide their mounts. With a bank loan which I paid back monthly, we purchased the necessary horses, saddles, bridles, blankets, and saddle bags and allocated them to the various stations in the sector as conditions dictated. Most of our horses were three to five year olds, heavier boned and larger than quarterhorses, brown or black so they could not be seen readily at night. They were picked for their disposition; as with people, the best looking are not necessarily the easiest to work with, and appearance does not help a bit when a man's life is at stake. The plan worked well, although after I was transferred to San Antonio, somebody in authority behind a desk decided it was not strictly regulation and put an end to it.

Experience in the outside force proved that positions in the Border Patrol were strictly for young men, with a sprinkling of knowledgeable officers who had the necessary initiative combined with good judgment. This was important because a large percentage of the force had to be stationed in units of two to five officers in locations where they were out of contact with headquarters. The El Paso Sector covered the country north to an easterly extension of the Colorado-New Mexico state line, and roughly eighty miles on either side of El Paso, much of which was extremely difficult to patrol because of the climate. Officers scouting the back country stayed out only two or three days unless they hit a hot trail; whereas officers covering outlying transportation routes in details of three or four would stay out for perhaps a week or ten days at a time, setting up camp where they could maintain surveillance over a road or stretch of railroad tracks. Staying alive in some of that border country was difficult enough without having to worry about apprehending lawbreakers as well. During the summer, the heat could be almost unbearable; lips would swell; the bottoms of one's feet would burn through the thickest-soled shoes; and some sort of protection to prevent second and third degree burns from reflected heat and light, as well as the direct rays of the sun, was almost mandatory. The cold in winter was equally bad. The men often took blankets to wrap up in when working the river, and I distinctly remember putting my gloves in my mouth because I was afraid the smugglers we were after might hear my teeth chattering. Even rain came in its most inhospitable forms: too much, too seldom, in torrential downpours that often brought hailstones, sometimes approaching the size of tennis balls. Around El Paso, winter storms were mostly sand, blowing like hell horizontally. In the city, especially before the streets were paved, it would be impossible to see half a block away in the daytime, even with the street lights turned on. If we were caught out in the open country in such a storm, we kept moving unless the sand was being blown so hard the horses would not face into it. Then all we could do would be to hole up until sundown in the lee of an abandoned shack, big rock or cut bank.

By the latter part of 1924 the El Paso force had been increased to about forty officers, which was not large in view of the work required and the fact that the majority of the new men needed months of training to reach peak efficiency. Giving them the indoctrination they needed made me appreciate all the more the experienced officers who had grown up in that country, who liked being on their own, and who functioned best when exposed to physical danger. Those who stayed in the Patrol had several other valuable qualities in common: they were honest, dependable, fearless, and seldom wasted a motion, functioning with unhurried calm because they knew exactly what they were doing. Bud Perry was a good example of the type of man needed in the Patrol before large areas of unoccupied country could be covered by airplanes, and radios supplied officers in the field with up-to-date information about the sections to which they were assigned. Perry was a soft-spoken, quiet mannered yet self-confident individual who neither looked for trouble nor ran away when it showed up. He was well into his forties when he joined the Service, after working as a hired gun for one of the big cattle outfits. It was not unusual then for the major companies to have gunmen on their payrolls to protect their ranch hands from gunmen employed by other ranchers, because they were all stealing cattle from each other. Another good officer was Patrol Inspector Tisdale, who grew up in sheep ranching country and enlisted in the Army at the start of the war. He was what was known as an Army gambler. Every company had several who would get the uninitiated into poker games on paydays and relieve them of their money. Tisdale, however, waited until the gamblers got theirs, then he took them on. As a result, he ended up with two paydays every time the Army had one. He saved his money and was supposed to be independently wealthy by the time he was discharged at Fort Bliss, but he proved to be a good, reliable officer, and to my knowledge never gambled after joining the Border Patrol.

Some of the first Patrolmen were a little too quick with a gun, or given to drinking too much, too often, and had to be let out, but in the main we managed to pull the recruits into line, and several made outstanding officers. It took time to weed out the unfit, but not the dishonest. The others were proud of the organization, and those who yielded to temptation could not operate for long without being found out. Also, the schemes people became involved with then were seldom devious, and therefore were relatively easy to uncover. Throughout the twelve years or more I was in El Paso, only two Inspectors turned crooked, and that was during Prohibition. They were caught letting liquor go by, instead of turning the carriers over to Prohibition or Customs officers, and were allowed to resign with prejudice because we were unable to obtain enough information on them to prosecute. One of the pair almost immediately started popping off about killing me because he had been fired unjustly, so Perry made it a point to meet the man in the office when he showed up to claim his final paycheck. Bud walked over to him and said, "I understand you've been making a lot of big talk about how you're going to kill the boss. Well, he's a young man with two little children, and I'm an old guy without a family, so it doesn't make any difference if I get killed. If you feel like killing somebody, go for your gun!" That fellow could not say loud enough or fast enough that he had never thought of such a thing, and the last glimpse of him was when he backed out of the office with all the starch of a wet noodle. He, like others who knew Bud Perry, wanted no part of him in a gunfight.

When the word reached Pete Torres, a fine Spanish-American officer from New Mexico who spoke English with a slight accent and fluent border Spanish, he was equally determined to take care of the ex-Patrolman. Pete was a sinewy, leathery type, rather tall and dark complexioned, with the strong face and high, prominent cheekbones of some Indian forebear. When he smiled, which was seldom, his entire face lit up, but he was a loaded deadly weapon on two feet when he came to my office and quietly said, "*Jefe.* You tell me to, I keel the sonofabeetch!" He was an extremely valuable man on the river, for he thought like a Mexican and looked like one. He could meander through the Mexican sections without arousing suspicion, especially at night, and he had no nerves at all. He may have been a little quick on the trigger, but his actions in every shooting match during which smugglers were killed always proved justified by the circumstances. The men had to be good shots, for if they were not, they did not last long. During one evening from our swing on the front porch, I heard three gunfights going on at the same

Border Patrol 97

time, in each of which my men were involved. As I recall, twenty-four smugglers and two officers were killed and several officers were wounded in gunfights on the river between 1924 and 1926. That sort of thing did little to improve my opinion of the value of Prohibition.

Ex-Texas Ranger and Cavalry Scout Miles Scannel when he was assistant chief of the U.S. Border Patrol in 1924 at the Marfa sub-District. Miles was killed by Mexican outlaws in 1929.
[SMITHERS COLLECTION, HUMANITIES RESEARCH CENTER
THE UNIVERSITY OF TEXAS AT AUSTIN]

Above, patrolmen charge smugglers near Presidio, Texas in 1928. Below, the apprehended aliens are taken into custody.

[SMITHERS COLLECTION, HUMANITIES RESEARCH CENTER
THE UNIVERSITY OF TEXAS AT AUSTIN]

SAN ANTONIO

XI

DOWN ON THE RIO GRANDE

✻ WITHIN TWO YEARS the Border Patrol in the El Paso District was a healthy, coordinated outfit that was beginning to inspire a considerable amount of public confidence. The officers were well trained and disciplined; they could be counted on in any tight spot they encountered; generally, they reflected the efforts expended to set up a model for the nationwide, responsible division of the Immigration Service we hoped the Patrol would become. Walter E. Carr, the District Director in California, had taken almost as active a part in the establishment of the Border Patrol as George Harris, the man probably most responsible for providing the initial impetus necessary to put the new organization into successful operation. As a result, the Patrol in California progressed almost as rapidly as it did in El Paso, and proved to be every bit as deserving of public support. The story in the San Antonio District during the same period, however, was quite different. There, due to politics in and out of the Service, the Patrol's primary accomplishment was to gain a bad reputation practically the entire length of the Rio Grande.

Influence peddling and the spoils system have been more a way of life in Texas than perhaps any other state in the Union, the result, I suspect, of the thousands of miles of onetime practically uninhabited country brought under a semblance of control only by tough, determined ranchers who had little or no help to start with from local or federal law officers. To survive, as well as to protect their property against rustlers, renegades, and raiders from below the border, the successful early settlers had to shoot first and ask questions later. To continue to hold onto what they had acquired with such difficulty, they and their descendants, with the assistance of equally tough hired hands, enlarged and consolidated their islands of rugged individualism into self-sufficient empires, giving little more than lip service to outside authority.

The first effective law enforcement officers along the Rio Grande were counterparts of these early ranchers: the determined Texas

Rangers, who had to be tough to tame the country and its inhabitants. Not surprisingly, growing numbers of federal law enforcement officers who served the expanding population received little help from either local officials or the Rangers; the federals found their efforts often triggered confrontations with landowners long accustomed to being laws unto themselves. Right or wrong, many felt they had the right to keep what they had by whatever means they could. Resorting to less deadly but equally devastating methods of preserving their positions, they turned to circumvention of the laws through pressure, favoritism, and eventually through political corruption. In such a climate, the life of any law officer or organization was apt to be both difficult and short. It was therefore understandable that the district director of the Immigration Service in the San Antonio District was a political appointee instead of an officer who had come up through the ranks, as was the case elsewhere. Also, it followed that he allowed personnel under him to carry on in any way they saw fit, so long as their actions did not interfere with his prerogatives, and that beyond recruiting enough men to bring the Border Patrol up to its authorized strength after funds were appropriated, he did nothing to build an organization. As a consequence, operations were slipshod; the men were disrespectful to their superiors as well as to each other, inefficient in what work they did and careless in their appearance, showing up for duty out of uniform or wearing only parts of it, which was worse.

To clean up the situation in this district, I was transferred to the San Antonio headquarters as Chief Patrol Inspector in June of 1926 and was promoted to Assistant Superintendent of the Border Patrol on my arrival. This was both a substantial advancement and a tremendous challenge, for the San Antonio District extended north to the Texas-Oklahoma state line. Sector offices were located in Del Rio, Laredo, Brownsville, and San Antonio; officers were also stationed at many of the small towns in the Rio Grande Valley where traffic warranted. Usually only two men were at a station, but some places there were four or more. A detail of seven men checking traffic twenty-four hours a day was stationed at Falfurrias, for example. It was some distance from the border, but it was on a main road leading directly from the river, so all northbound traffic funneled through there. With about one hundred and twenty-five men scattered over several hundred miles of river, plenty of opportunity existed for trouble to develop for the Border Patrol during its formative years, especially with the activities of the military and the rough though effective methods of the Texas Rangers as examples. Army patrols along the Rio Grande were concerned only with the possibility of invasion of Mexican forces. The Texas Rangers, as state police, were involved with individuals breaking Texas statutes, including liquor runners and bandits who operated on both sides of the Rio stealing cattle, killing people, and doing various other things over which the Border Patrol had no authority. Neither the Army nor the Rangers had any interest or authority in the enforcement of federal laws, such as those concerned with immigration, although during the Mexican disturbances all law enforcement officers became mixed up with them to some extent.

Many early Patrolmen were acquainted with the Texas Rangers and their activities and started to emulate them despite the fact that the Patrol was dealing with the general public, not criminals. It makes a lot of difference whether an officer is in a shoot-out with a bunch of rustlers or winnowing out a small percentage of aliens engaged in unlawful activities. It took considerable indoctrinating to convince some of the inspectors they were not chasing outlaws, and we never did get it out of the heads of all of them, for we had to discharge several for being too rough. A good percentage had not been well trained, so that once in a while conditions arose that became serious before either the sector or district offices were aware of what was going on. Not all of the problems were obvious, and a few would have proved very injurious to the Patrol had there been any publicity. One involved a Mexican arrested as a smuggler, whose case was referred back to our office by the judge when it came to trial because there was no evidence against the man beyond his confession. During the ensuing investigation it developed that the man's confession was all the evidence in the case. Two officers had apprehended him near the river in what appeared to be rather suspicious circumstances, had tied his feet together, and had dragged him into the water to conduct an interrogation. Every time they asked and he denied that he was a smuggler, they jerked his feet out from under him. After enough dunkings, they obtained what they considered a satisfactory admission of guilt and took the fellow in.

Making something over to secure the results desired is a good deal more difficult than starting out fresh. District Director Whalen and I put in many grueling hours of overtime in straightening out the district and putting the Border Patrol on the proper track. Over a year was required to pull the men together and build up their morale after the elimination of officers who could not (or would not) perform their duties properly. The job would have taken considerably longer without the assistance of about half a dozen officers from El Paso who put in formal applications for transfer to San Antonio when I moved. They were top men who could be placed in charge of units, men like Fletcher Rawls, who had served as a Senior Patrol Inspector at Fabens, Las Cruces and on many temporary details; their applications were approved promptly because the need for such men was so urgent. Another major contributor was Clyde Campbell, my erstwhile duckhunting companion from El Paso. As Assistant District Director, Clyde had been extremely unhappy about the way the District was being run, so we had his enthusiastic cooperation from the start. Also, he was willing to take on many of Mr. Whalen's responsibilities temporarily, as well as give me every bit of help I needed while we endeavored to solve the immediate problems of the Patrol in the Del Rio, Brownsville and Laredo Sectors.

Most of my inspection trips through the district were made in a government car, my first stop usually being Del Rio for a couple of days, Laredo for three or four more, then back to San Antonio or Brownsville. The trips involved a great deal of driving through open, uninhabited country, but they were the only way to keep track of what the men were doing, including those who were assigned to strategic points away from district and sector offices and who operated largely on their own. During the trips, I made it a point to approach each check point in a way that would enable me to determine whether or not the officers were on the job, assess their demeanor and personal appearance and note the state of their uniforms and equipment before they knew who I was. In the sector offices, particularly when notice of my arrival had been sent in advance, the chief patrol inspector would arrange to have the men in so I could talk to them collectively, answer any questions they might have, and emphasize what we wanted done in given situations. Afterwards, I would review assignments with the chief patrol inspector, ascertain the results being obtained by his men at outlying stations, what his problems were, if any, what he needed in the way of additional personnel or equipment, and go through the officers' reports. I also made it a habit to check each sector's vehicles and equipment, talk with the mechanic to find out what his problems were, and make sure the men were taking proper care of the vehicles they used.

The Del Rio Sector included the cattle and sheep country of the upper Rio Grande Valley, where few laborers were needed and the incentive to smuggle Mexican aliens was not great. The initial opposition to the Patrol could be laid almost entirely at the door of one resident: Representative John Nance Garner, later vice-president of the United States under Franklin D. Roosevelt. During a joint inspection trip out of San Antonio, District Director Whalen and I stopped at the Garner home to get acquainted; we wanted to enlist Mr. Garner's cooperation or at least obtain his agreement to remain neutral. Also, Mr. Whalen had been transferred to San Antonio through the efforts of the Assistant Secretary of Labor, who was a close friend, so he felt he should give service to the more important political officials in his district. District Director Whalen was a good administrator, somewhat easy going, and rather than back up the Border Patrol against complaints, he was inclined to have the men soft pedal their activities. On the other hand, I was anxious to bring the Patrol up to what it should be as quickly as possible, and I was not inclined to make calls that did not relate directly to matters at hand. I was also probably a little rough on the men, so working with Mr. Whalen was valuable training for me and together we made a good team.

Mr. Garner had a large cattle and sheep ranch near Uvalde, plus some acreage where the hunting was reportedly excellent throughout the year despite laws existing to the contrary. He lived in a large, old-fashioned, two-story white colonial home built on a low hill overlooking a long, open pasture some distance from the main road. He was an erect, vigorous man with a weathered face and white hair, a trifle on the chunky side, but an impressive figure when standing on the wide porch overlooking his ranch. At home, Representative Garner customarily wore a dark shirt and Levis tucked into the tops of high-heeled cowboy boots; outside, he added a large Stetson with four dents pressed into the peak of the crown. His speech was Southern, but his mannerisms were strictly Western, and though he was outspoken and very definite about his likes and dislikes, he was a most congenial gentleman of the old school. After ringing the front door bell the first time we visited the ranch, District Director Whalen and I were invited into a large, comfortably furnished living room. Once we were seated near a huge fireplace and drinks had been served, Mr. Garner proceeded to speak frankly and pointedly about conditions as he saw them on the border. He told us in no uncertain terms that he had very little use for the work the Patrol was doing and would make the most of every complaint coming his way to embarrass Republican incumbents in Washington. While we were there, several of his cronies from neighboring ranches stopped in and joined freely in the discussion, indicating they shared his views.

In the months that followed I stopped at the ranch several times, becoming well enough acquainted with Mr. Garner to go into Patrol matters which had been referred to him by his constituents. When he understood what we were trying to do, and the need for a Patrol in other areas along the border, his attitude changed considerably and I found him reasonable to deal with. He even changed to the point where he began closing our discussions with, "Well, just don't pay any attention to it. I'll write something to cool them off." If the complaint were legitimate and of any importance, however, he always followed up on it personally. He eventually became a strong advocate of the Border Patrol whenever an appropriations bill came up in Congress, and he even went so far as to extend several invitations to me to go hunting (out of season) on his property, offers which pressing matters elsewhere somehow always prevented my being able to accept.

Opposition to the Border Patrol in the Brownsville Sector was considerable and stemmed from ranchers and farmers in the lower Rio Grande Valley who had benefitted greatly before the Patrol entered the picture by using Mexican wetbacks to plant and harvest their crops. The laborers were paid practically nothing, and such exorbitant prices were charged for food, clothing and other essentials at ranch commisaries that they were usually in debt to their employers by the end of their stay. Inspectors picking up illegal entrants literally by the thousands and sending them back across the line aroused the resentment of the growers, and they were not reluctant to register complaints that would make trouble for the Patrol. To make matters worse, the head of the Republican Party in Texas resided in the Brownsville Sector and made himself accessible to anyone with a real of imaginary complaint to make about Patrol activities.

The Brownsville Sector was by far the best organized in the district when I became assistant superintendent, though that was not saying much. Considering the others, however, it was a good deal, and all the credit went to Chief Patrol Inspector Portus Gay, a long-time resident of Brownsville and former Texas Ranger. In an effort to cope with the wetbacks pouring into the country during the growing season, he kept very few men in the sector office, scattering the better part of his force along the river as far up as Rio Grande City. Their efficiency and reputation were slightly better than elsewhere, but so much feeling existed against them at the time of my first inspection trip, that their morale was shaky or nonexistent, and it showed in their sloppy appearance. The lack of cooperation from residents and the overwhelming numbers of illegal entrants contributed greatly to the men's discouragement. Officers at one station reconciled themselves to their difficult situation by setting a daily quota of wetbacks to be picked up. Once that number had been reached, they quit looking, knowing inspectors at the ports of entry would be unable to process more out of the country, a procedure involving not much more than putting the aliens back across the river after identifying data were taken.

Shortly after transferring from El Paso, and before becoming known to more than a few men at the Brownsville headquarters, I pulled up to the highway check point near Falfurrias late one afternoon and purposely stopped a few feet beyond the inspector on duty. He approached my car belligerently and said, "Where the hell do you think you're going?" To his decided discomfiture my response shot back, "Well, I'm the new Border Patrol superintendent in this district, and I am returning home to San Antonio. Do you always greet everybody the way you did me?" The incident must have filtered rapidly through channels, for reports of discourtesies on the part of patrolmen were noticeably rare from then on.

During another inspection trip down river from Laredo, I stopped to check the station at Rio Grande City. While there I met a new Patrol inspector who was stationed at Brownsville and looking for a ride home, so I offered him a lift. He was an extremely talkative young man, and before the outskirts of Rio Grande City had dropped behind us, he was bragging about the Patrol, what a great organization it was, and how glad he was to be in it. Then he said, "You know what makes this Patrol so great? Well, it's because we have all Texans in it. I've never yet seen a Yankee with enough sense to come in out of the rain, and if we had a bunch of them in the Patrol, they'd screw up the works until it wouldn't amount to anything!" He kept rattling away without any encouragement from me as the miles rolled by, so I went on driving, nodding occasionally, and letting him do the talking. By the time we neared Brownsville he had apparently unwound somewhat, for he turned to me and said, "Well Mr. Perkins, Don't you agree that these Texans are what make the Border Patrol?" I answered, "You could be right," to which he nodded, pleased with my apparent agreement. Then, realizing he should be polite and allow me an opportunity to say something, he asked, "Where were you born?" When I answered "Wisconsin," he almost slid off the car seat, and at the Brownsville office he could not disappear fast enough. For two years he managed to be the only officer in the sector consistently elsewhere when I came through town, but reports of his progress indicated he was developing into one of the better reviewing officers on the force.

Regular monthly inspection visits to every station in the district, plus problems involving officers and liquor, women, goofing off and falsifying time reports, use of government cars for personal business, men acting as bouncers at local affairs, exceeding authority, and similar forms of human dereliction of duty kept me on the road at least half of my waking hours during my nearly four years as assistant superintendent of the Border Patrol in the San Antonio District. Actually there were few instances where severe disciplinary action had to be taken, and after eighteen officers resigned rather than wait for charges to be presented against them, we had few serious problems. None of my trips were made on a regular basis, however, until the Laredo Sector was cleaned up.

Border Patrolmen with captured smugglers handcuffed near Presidio, Texas.

[SMITHERS COLLECTION, HUMANITIES RESEARCH CENTER
THE UNIVERSITY OF TEXAS AT AUSTIN]

XII

PROBLEMS AND SOLUTIONS

✱ WITHIN AN HOUR after walking out of the hotel on my first inspection trip to the Laredo Sector, I knew there was trouble ahead. Laredo was a strictly Mexican town, Spanish being spoken more than English, and probably ninety percent of the people were either Mexican or of Mexican descent. Except for the new buildings, practically every structure was adobe and, as in Mexico, narrow sidewalks were all that separated house walls from eighteen to twenty-foot wide streets. When I entered the Patrol office the first time, three men were lounging around smoking, swapping yarns, and laughing. After introducing myself, they stopped joking, but they continued to sprawl on the desks or lean back in chairs with their feet up. I assumed one of the men was a visitor because of his casual dress, but I soon discovered he was a Patrol inspector like the other two, who had on random combinations of regular and uniform clothing.

It was mid-afternoon before I met the man responsible for the lack of discipline and the disgraceful manner in which the force was functioning. The chief Patrol inspector proved to be a rough, tough, tobacco-chewing, "if they don't talk, work 'em over with a six-shooter" bully, weighing well over two hundred and fifty pounds. The minute he lumbered into the office he made it clear he had *political* connections, and no matter what I tried to do, no changes were going to be made in the way *his* boys were operating. For the time being, I decided the best thing to do was go right along with him and to develop information outside the office about the men's qualifications and local Patrol activities.

Laredo residents at that time were very dubious about Americans, especially American officers, as I suspected my first morning on the way from the hotel to the office. My suspicions were confirmed when I learned the only Anglo on the police force was the chief himself. If it had not been for my brother Lyle's having lived there for years, and his being well liked, I would have had an impossible task in becoming acquainted with the more influential residents and city officials and in establishing contacts of value to the Service. However, Lyle not only knew everybody of consequence, he knew "who" was "who" and why, socially as well as politically. He also understood the operations of the Immigration Service and was thoroughly familiar with the rumors around town regarding the Border Patrol.

Lyle, eighteen months younger than I, followed me to El Paso after graduating from high school and found temporary work for about a year until his examination for the Customs Service led to his appointment at Laredo. After working as a Customs officer, he went into the insurance business, acted as a deputy U.S. Marshal on the side, speculated in real estate and oil, and was president of a savings and loan association when he died in 1943. With his help in opening doors, it did not take much digging to learn that Immigration officials were mixed up with the local smuggling of aliens and contraband from Mexico, and that their reputation for catching aliens had been established through cooperation with the smuggling gangs. Officers involved in these activities would allow European aliens to be brought across the river, where the smugglers would forcibly relieve them of all their money and valuables, then instruct them to hide in the brush and not move until their next guide appeared unless they wanted to risk apprehension by Border Patrolmen. The smugglers would then report the location of the aliens to the Patrol office. In short order, they would be picked up, examined and deported, never realizing how thoroughly they had been duped; a few more alien apprehensions would be credited to the Laredo office; and the smugglers would have been paid for transporting the illegal entrants, immune from prosecution.

Smuggling turned out to be a big time operation in the Laredo Sector, all sorts of contraband, especially liquor, being funneled from Mexico into Duval County, then north through San Diego, the county seat. Pack trains of as many as sixty animals, escorted by five or six wranglers and up to ten armed men, moved the goods, and while they were not exactly inconspicuous, finding residents willing to talk about them proved almost impossible. Knowing that trails used by trains of such size would be well worn, scouting details were sent out to cut for sign south of Duval County, reports coming back that trains appeared to be moving through about twice a month. When the approximate dates were established and a train was due, a joint detail of twelve Border Patrol and Customs officers moved into the cattle country halfway between San Diego and the Rio Grande. In the area we selected, the trains were traveling through a huge pasture much too flat to afford us adequate cover close in, but with a new north fence line ten miles or more in length. To avoid alerting the train's armed guards, we split and holed up well away from the trail, planning to move under cover of darkness. To keep track of the train, probably the first time outside the military, we borrowed two field telephones from the Army, and hooked one near each end of the top strand of the barbed wire fence, after making sure it was intact. By calling through every fifteen minutes, beginning at sundown, we could determine if the wire had been cut, and approximately when, without exposing ourselves. At two in the morning of our first night in the pasture, the line was dead. By prearrangement, both groups of officers mounted up and started riding cautiously towards the opposite end of the fence. At the break were fresh tracks indicating a large train was involved, so we followed at a good distance, preparing to close in at dawn. When the sky began to lighten, we sent an experienced tracker ahead to scout the train and lay of the land. In less than half an hour he rode back into view, signaling for us to move forward to the foot of a low hill. When we reached him, he reported the train had camped for the night beside a water hole on the other side of the hill, and the fourteen men with it were asleep—not a guard anywhere! We again divided into two groups, six officers circling the camp to move in from the opposite side. When everybody had been allowed sufficient time to position themselves as planned, the detail across from us charged the train at a dead run. At the sound of their first pistol shots, we converged from our side, and before the smugglers knew what was happening, we were standing over them, guns ready. A few tried to resist and were shot for their enthusiasm, but the majority of the men were tied up and taken to jail. They were eventually convicted, and that was the last pack train of any size to carry contraband through that part of the country.

During the latter part of my two-week preliminary investigation in Laredo, sworn statements from Immigration Service and Patrol personnel, as well as outsiders having knowledge of what was going on, were taken with the assistance of a stenographer brought in from the San Antonio office. Although I was aware of being shadowed continuously, more than enough evidence was obtained to warrant the full-scale housecleaning which followed. Within forty-eight hours of my return to San Antonio, action was initiated against the ringleaders of the unlawful operations in Laredo, and as a result the Chief Patrol Inspector and two of his accomplices came in, offering to resign if they were not prosecuted. Since we did not have the sort of evidence which would have convicted them in court, their resignations were accepted, effective immediately. When word of what had happened reached Laredo, additional resignations started rolling in. Some of the men who had cooperated, and whose testimony showed that they had been forced to go along with the mess, were transferred to other sectors. Without exception, they made good at their new stations, but almost half of the twenty-eight officers stationed in Laredo were fired or quit.

Duval County continued to be a real sore spot to the Border Patrol for years because of one man's power. He not only controlled politics in the entire county, permitting open gambling and low-class houses of prostitution providing big payoffs were made to him, but he had considerable influence in the surrounding counties. From his headquarters next door to the county courthouse in San Diego, he appointed sheriffs, judges, and all the local officials, the voters merely going through the motions of electing the candidates he wanted. When the Laredo cleanup began, nearly every Patrolman in the sector was either mixed up in his manipulations or too scared to say anything. It turned out there were no inspectors stationed at San Diego, and when I inquired the reason, and one of the men said, "Archie doesn't allow them," I hit the ceiling. Parr considered himself absolutely independent of Texas and United States laws, while I believed that Border Patrolmen should be able to go anywhere within the scope of federal laws spelling out their responsibilities, without regard to local regulations. I stewed over that situation all during my initial investigations in Laredo, knowing a solution had to be found or the Border Patrol would ultimately become ineffective. Back in San Antonio, I went over the Patrol roster and selected eighteen or twenty inspectors who had been Texas Rangers and had not been seen in Duval County for several years; all were experienced, well-disciplined fighters who knew the country. One or two at a time, as inconspicuously as possible, they converged on Laredo. When all were present and accounted for, we moved on the bawdy houses of Duval County. Within twenty-four hours, we systematically picked up every illegal alien, Mexican prostitute and otherwise, and cleared out. It did not have a lasting effect on Archie, or his family, but by the same token nobody else ever tried to keep the Border Patrol out of any county, city, building or office it considered necessary to enter.

One of the first things I did after obtaining a clear picture of what was going on in Laredo, was to put in for the transfer of Bud Perry, who had been my Assistant Chief Patrol Inspector in El Paso, for with him in the office, there would be one individual I could trust absolutely. He was put in charge of the sector pending the assignment of a new Chief Patrol Inspector, and he helped immensely during the ensuing months in digging up and eliminating one connection after another with criminals, smugglers in Mexico, and political bosses in neighboring counties. Perry was the most loyal assistant anyone could want, although there was a time right after he joined the Patrol when I had serious doubts about being able to keep him. He started drinking for some reason, and his absences from duty lengthened until he finally disappeared for nearly a week on a colossal binge. When he showed up in the office, with a man-sized hangover, his first remark to me was a rather belligerent, "Well, I came in so you could fire me." Ignoring that, I sat back to give him a good looking over, then said, "Perry, you're too good an officer for the Service to lose. We need you, so go home and sober up. Then come back and we'll talk. And bring your wife, so she'll know what is going on." Bud was a different man when he and Mrs.

Perry walked into my office the next afternoon, and we were able to have a real heart-to-heart talk about his job, and where he was going. I told him if he would promise to leave liquor alone, I would ignore his dereliction from duty and give him one last chance to stay in the Patrol. With his promise, I handed him a blank form to sign as a request for his annual leave, to cover his absence. Then I leaned across my desk, studied each of them in turn, and said, "You both understand: this must be the absolute end of the drinking." It was, too, for until he retired Bud had the reputation in the Laredo Sector of being an excellent Assistant Chief Patrol Inspector.

Until comparatively recently, the only proof of citizenship many individuals had was the location shown on their baptismal certificates, a situation not unknown to smugglers. Therefore, it was assumed to be something more than coincidence when, within the space of a few months, over twenty newcomers to Laredo were found to be carrying baptismal certificates signed by the Catholic priest at Meyer, a tiny coal mining village about twenty miles up river. On the assumption that alien smugglers had adopted another twist to their racket, instructions were issued for all Patrol Inspectors to cross check the stories of every individual producing a Meyer certificate. The first break in the case came when a locally known prostitute with one of the certificates was determined to be a Mexican alien. When she was brought in for interrogation, she admitted the certificates were being sold by the priest at Meyer for twenty dollars each. During my next visit to Laredo, Bud Perry asked me to speak to the bishop in the hope that the situation could be corrected before further investigation confirmed existing evidence and it became necessary for the priest to be taken into custody and held over for trial.

The good bishop and I had become rather well acquainted during several lengthy discussions of mutual problems, and I felt sure he would find some solution short of our having to prosecute, if our suspicions were substantiated. He was most thoughtful while I told him what had been uncovered, then remarked, "Of course, he might not be the person you want," to which I agreed. After revolving the large ring on his left hand for several minutes without speaking, he placed a hand firmly on each arm of the heavy chair in which he was sitting and stood up. With no expression whatsoever on his face, but the growing suggestion of a smile in his eyes, he said, "Mr. Perkins, you know I am glad to assist the Service in any way possible, but unless I am greatly mistaken, the priest at Meyer is either about to leave, or is already on his way to a small missionary outpost, offhand I don't recall where. If you find it necessary to obtain testimony from him when your investigation is completed, please let me know, and I will make arrangements accordingly. Now, if there is nothing else requiring our consideration, may I offer you a glass of wine, or something stronger, from the cellar?" The bishop had an excellent stock in that cellar, as I well knew from previous visits. For some time I had kidded with him that becoming a priest was something I should consider, since he seemed to have the finest liquor supply in town, despite Prohibition, and a darned good housekeeper, too. We always agreed, however, that staying with the employer I had would probably be better for everyone concerned.

By the fall of 1928, the Border Patrol was functioning effectively enough in the San Antonio District to have reduced the number of illegal Mexican aliens in towns and cities located one to two hundred miles from the border. With more manpower available, we began assessing situations farther afield and discovered many illegal entrants moving south at the onset of winter were escaping apprehension by stopping short of areas where the Patrol was known to be active. We also found that numerous Mexican prostitutes, who had openly admitted at one time or another they were not citizens, were plying their trade in Dallas and Fort Worth. Until passage of the Literacy Act in 1917, a statute of limitations (in most cases of three years) applied to illegal aliens in the United States. In addition to stopping the entry of large numbers of Mexican peons, most of whom were illiterate, the Literacy Act eliminated the time period beyond which illegal entrants could not be deported. Because it also erased established immunity from deportation for certain undesirable classes, specifically including prostitutes and pimps, we decided to make a two-week drive on the brothels in Dallas and

Fort Worth. To assure maximum effectiveness for our efforts, I gathered every scrap of information available from discreet friends in San Antonio concerning each city's officials, major organizations, hotels, bars and bawdy houses.

Most of the police officers in Fort Worth were reported to be anywhere from undependable to downright crooked, but the force in Dallas was said to have a good reputation, and the administration to be free from graft. I also learned the Ku Klux Klan was still very much a factor in both cities, although enforcement of laws and defeats at the polls had resulted in a sizeable drop in its membership. To be on the safe side, I secured a letter of introduction to the Grand Dragon in Dallas from the head of the Klan in San Antonio. To cover the other side of the picture, I also obtained a letter from the bishop of the San Antonio Diocese to his counterpart in Dallas. When everything was set, eight of us left for Dallas, including Kight, Rawls, Tisdale, and four other officers who had put in for transfers to San Antonio shortly after I was assigned there. They drove up in three Patrol cars and a Patrol wagon, and I took my government-assigned car. On our arrival, the chief of police turned over three of his patrol cars, with drivers, as support vehicles, and that night with a policeman and Patrol inspector in each car we commended raiding establishments patronized by Mexicans. During our sweep we arrested over four hundred aliens, including forty or fifty prostitutes who angrily testified they had been making payoffs to the officials to leave them alone, and what was the big idea? Having arrived at Laredo, the prostitutes, pimps and criminals were formally deported, and the rest were given "voluntary returns" to Mexico.

After Dallas had been cleaned out, we conducted two or three raids into Fort Worth, but they were not so successful; word of our coming apparently had leaked out. Nobody seemed to know where the Mexican prostitutes had gone, so I decided to lean on one from San Antonio who had been picked up in our final raid in Dallas and released because she was a citizen. Taking a policeman with me, I went to the house where she was working and asked her where the women in Fort Worth had gone. She would not tell me, so I instructed the policeman to put her in jail pending deportation proceedings. She flew into a rage, swearing at me and yelling in between cuss words, "You know I'm an American citizen! You can't deport me!" When she hesitated to catch her breath, I said, "Well, you have no proof of it, and I don't know it. Now, Officer, take her to the car." With a chance to mull that over, she decided to cooperate and told me the women had gone to a small town outside of Fort Worth to stay out of our way. Before we went after them, I presented my letters of introduction to the bishop and Grand Dragon, and asked them who could be relied on to help us in the town where we were going. Both told me the officials were crooked and in cahoots with the underworld, and no one but the constable could be trusted. Amusingly enough as it turned out, he was neither a KKK nor a Catholic. Armed with the constable's address on the outskirts of town, our entourage left Dallas. Close to midnight the men pulled up to wait on a side road about half a mile from the constable's home while I drove on to request his assistance. About two in the morning we raided the houses where he indicated the Mexican prostitutes from Fort Worth were staying, rounding up nearly fifteen women plus several of their pimps. As soon as they were loaded into the Patrol wagon and on their way to San Antonio, the rest of us went to the hotel for some much-needed sleep.

Shortly before noon, while I was dressing, the telephone in my room rang and I was informed the town's chief of police was in the lobby asking to see me. Curious as to what he had in mind following the previous night's activities, I went downstairs to meet him. With the amenities taken care of, I found out all he apparently wanted was to know if he could be of any help to us, for when I told him, "No" and thanked him, he turned on his heel and left. That his visit was not as innocent as it appeared on the surface was proven within ten or fifteen minutes when a local attorney sat down uninvited at my table in the dining room. Abruptly he stated that if I did not let him speak to the women we had arrested, he would file writs of *habeas corpus* and have them freed. Obviously he was not aware they were on their way to San Antonio and was doing his best to find out where they had been taken, so I told him to go ahead and turned my attention to what was left of my late, cold breakfast. Before I had finished, the inspector on duty in the San Antonio office called to say our truck had arrived, the necessary warrants had been secured by telegraph, and the women were in jail awaiting deportation hearings.

As everything was under control in San Antonio, I stopped in Waco on the way home. When I learned that a large percentage of the city's Negro population was out of work because Mexican wetbacks had moved in and taken their jobs, I arranged to speak to the congregation of the largest church in their district. After telling the congregation how the Mexicans were smuggling in, and why, one of the deacons tipped me off to where a large number of wetbacks were working. We also had the complete cooperation of the entire Negro population of Waco and its vicinity for several years thereafter. Periodically, we made two or three week raids in the Fort Worth-Dallas-Waco area for some time. They always resulted in our picking up large numbers of illegal Mexican aliens, but at no time did we ever secure such wholesale cooperation as we did during our first drive through Dallas.

After over three years of concentrated attention on my part to set the Patrol in the San Antonio District on the right track, it became obvious to more people than me that the men were doing their work well. Ranchers, citrus grove owners, and operators of commercial truck gardens began to have field crews picked up almost as rapidly as they could be put to work, and vented their displeasure by writing their Congressmen and other individuals in government offices in Washington, D.C. These officials responded by doing everything they could to put an end to activities of the Border Patrol. The matter became so controversial that Kenneth L. Roberts, a nationally-known writer, arranged to make a first-hand analysis of the situation. Orders came through from Washington for Mr. Roberts to be shown every courtesy when he arrived in San Antonio, so I was detailed to take him on a personally conducted tour through the district. After several days of meetings with headquarters personnel, we drove to Brownsville, where I arranged interviews for him with a number of residents and Border Patrol officers, as well as D. W. Brewster, the Inspector in Charge of the Immigration office there. Then I took him out to visit a number of the truck farms and citrus groves so he would have an opportunity to speak with growers on the scene. From there, we went on to Rio Grande City, Laredo, Eagle Pass and Del Rio, following much the same program. At Devils River we were met by the El Paso Patrol Superintendent, who took Mr. Roberts on a similar journey through to Yuma.

Following his return to Washington, D.C., a series of articles by Kenneth Roberts appeared in the *Saturday Evening Post* which went a long way to cement relations of the Border Patrol with people living near our international boundaries. His obvious grasp of conditions on the border was personally very satisfying, since I had been on the verge of pneumonia by the time we reached Laredo, and exposing him to an unprejudiced view of what was going on in the district had been almost more than I could manage. The articles were gratifying to read, too, for they meant that the efforts of a great many men in the Border Patrol, the Immigration Service, and in public and private life, were proving worthwhile. That knowledge enabled me to leave San Antonio satisfied the job I was sent there to do had been accomplished.

Above, four Border Patrolmen were watching for a crossing in the Rio Grande at night near Brownsville, Texas. This was in 1935 after the repeal of prohibition. Below, three smugglers are relieved of their guns after an arrest made south of Tucson, Arizona in 1926 during prohibition.

[SMITHERS COLLECTION, HUMANITIES RESEARCH CENTER THE UNIVERSITY OF TEXAS AT AUSTIN]

TIJUANA

XIII

A DINNER IN TIJUANA

✱ WE GATHERED at Nacho's Restaurant on Avenida Revolución just across the border — a place where Mexicans and Americans met and mingled every day. An eight-piece mariachi band in the traditional tight-fitting black pants, black jackets and buff-colored sombreros was playing as we entered. Señor Fernando Calzada Jiménez, Chief of Mexican Immigration at the San Ysidro port of entry, had sent me the invitation in November in the name of himself and his staff and had assembled all available men from both offices with their wives — nearly forty people in all.

The warmth of Christmas was all about us. Outside, the streets shone with lighted decorations; inside, two heavy gold-framed mirrors hanging on facing walls of the main dining area wished us all "MERRY CHRISTMAS AND HAPPY NEW YEAR 1954" and "FELIZ ANO NUEVO."

The gathering was without precedent on the international border. An official of the Mexican government was recognizing the retirement of his United States counterpart. There was some evidence of a language barrier, for United States and Mexican Immigration officers working at the border are not expected to be masters of both languages, but the atmosphere of festive informality removed constraint. When it was time for the speeches, Rodolfo Valladolid would translate. Now there was the hum of relaxed conversation.

When we were seated and waiting for dinner to be served, I listened to the nostalgic melodies the band was playing and studied the familiar faces of the men seated around the long table. Several had spent most of their lives on the border. All were fine officers and valued friends. I wondered when, if ever, we would meet again. The support and cooperation given me over the years by people from both our countries had been responsible for much of my effectiveness. Don Taylor, for example, had been invaluable to me and would prove so to the new officer in charge. Traffic at San Ysidro was so heavy most of the time that it was essential to have a man like Don, who was a jack of all trades and could fill any position at the line. Officers like Bernie Berlin and Bill Bassett would be needed as well. They were exceptionally reliable and highly skilled at reading people and sizing them up. Bernie certainly seemed to be enjoying his conversation with Rudy Valladolid — such a friendly, diplomatic individual and an excellent contact man from the Mexican Immigration Office. Rudy and Charlie Birchfield made a fine team in keeping matters running smoothly between the two offices.

Charlie, of course, I had known longest of all. He was hired under the Passport Act in 1918 and was the only man present who was with me patrolling for smugglers all the way from Arizona to the Gulf of Mexico. It had been twenty years ago that he was so badly wounded in that gunfight outside of El Paso. His hearing had been seriously affected, so seriously that his life was jeopardized on patrols. Transfer to the International Bridge and then to the administrative force had worked out well for both of us. What a surprise it had been when I returned to San Ysidro after six years in Naval Intelligence during World War II to find that Charlie had transferred there from Calexico.

Then there was Moises Sánchez Aldana, the senior Mexican officer present in point of service. He was already on duty at Tijuana when I transferred from Texas in 1930. He and all the rest were my friends. Their history, their language, their customs were so deeply interwoven into the fabric of my life that words could not describe my feelings. I thought that perhaps everyone would understand, when it was my turn to rise, if I said something to the effect that I had become so attached to the border and its people that I was planning to spend the rest of my life on a ranch in the hills above the Tijuana Valley.

Dinners in Mexico are gracious and leisurely affairs, and as the white-coated waiters went about their business of serving the excellent dinner, my mind went back over the past twenty-four years, the problems and solutions which had brought me to this moment.

I could not help reflecting how much the picture had changed in that interval. In 1930 there were only three or four good inspectors among the fourteen officers on the force. To make matters worse, my predecessor was very unpopular with the public on both sides of the line, and especially with the Mexicans in Tijuana. There was a great deal of dissension and morale was nonexistent. Our building was unsatisfactory and the two-lane street outside made it difficult for the men to handle traffic. A man who had dominated the staff and arranged for my predecessor to be transferred threatened to "get" me too, but he did not succeed.

I remembered that I had made myself unpopular with the staff that first year by putting a stop to the practice of accepting liquor and presents at Christmas; other changes cost me more of their approval, but gradually the men came around and within a reasonably short period, they were pulling together in a manner that reflected favorably on the port. I tried to inculcate in the minds of the inspectors that they were dealing with people, not things, and that faulty judgment could affect the entire future of a man or woman. I spent hours behind the counter men and more hours watching the inspectors working outside to see how they were handling their jobs, trying to get them to listen sympathetically to everyone who came to them and to bring the doubtful cases to me. The effectiveness of this policy was reflected to some extent in the cordiality which I felt at the retirement party now going on.

Of course there was always pressure from people who wanted favors, from influential citizens who wanted their own way, even from people in Washington. There were always special problems to solve. Should Mrs. Carrillo, who needed special medical treatment, be allowed to come in and have her baby in the United States, thereby automatically producing one more American citizen? What could be done about a Mexican motorcycle patrolman, a friend of mine, who was shaking down patrons returning from the Agua Caliente racetrack? How could we manage to speed up the long lines of traffic at the border?

We worked hard at finding solutions, and when as an officer in Naval Intelligence I was called to active duty in 1940, I was able to leave without too much worry. On my return six years later, however, it was all to do over again. The drain on manpower during

A Dinner in Tijuana

the war had resulted in a deterioration in the calibre of men the Service had been able to secure, and once again the organization had to be rebuilt.

It had been rebuilt, slowly and painfully but surely. Now it was time to let somebody else take over.

At last Señor Calzada placed his napkin beside his plate and rose to speak. In gracious, soft-spoken Spanish he addressed his attentive listeners:

Honorable Señor Clifford A. Perkins, Compañeros Funcionarios de Migración, Señoras y Señores:

Otra vez encontramos en circunstancias similares, pagando un signo de honor y reconocimiento merecido cual que se ofrecen del Servicio de Migración Mexicano a un compañero íntimo que se retira desde deber activo después de que sembrando amistades profundas y sólidas durante sus ejercicios oficiales.

I found his words deeply moving: "We have met again in familiar surroundings to pay honor and give deserved recognition such as may be offered by the Mexican Immigration Service to a close and dear companion, retiring from active duty after having sowed deep and solid friendships during his years of official service.

"But a greater significance is attached to this occasion because we come here to bid farewell to a man who, in addition to his great merits as a high and efficient officer of the American Immigration has also provided a magnificent example of cordial friendship and human understanding of immigration problems on this border as well as of the good neighbor policy which has been well applied by our personnel on either side of the frontier.

"When the integrity of our systems and of our codes of protocol allow us the liberty to use our own judgments in the best interests of our two countries, a sustaining understanding will bring us to a basis of good faith and mutual comprehension.

"At this moment I am gripped by a great emotion on the departure of our good friend, Clifford A. Perkins, although his absence signifies for him a reward of peace and quiet made more enjoyable by the best sentiments of the heart and mind, a reward for work well done during a lifetime devoted to his home and his country.

"Unquestionably it is also true that his absence will leave a place of sadness in the hearts of all his friends who have long known the value of this good, honest, modest man whose virtues will make us forever remember him with deeply felt sentiments of affection.

"Mr. Perkins, on behalf of my personnel and myself, I rise to offer my toast, assuring you of our great desire for your personal happiness and for that of your family and giving testimony to my regard and my heartfelt friendship."

The sincere and generous compliment touched me deeply. There wasn't a word I would have changed in honoring Señor Calzada had our situations been reversed. It made me hope that when my race is over it will be said, as is often said of a thoroughbred, "At least he was always in there trying."

The International Boundary Gate at Calexico, California and Mexicali, Baja California, Mexico. United States is at the right, Mexico at the left. Picture made in 1935.

[SMITHERS COLLECTION, HUMANITIES RESEARCH CENTER
THE UNIVERSITY OF TEXAS AT AUSTIN]

On September 16, 1926 near Nogales, Arizona, Patrolman Frank Edgell induced about 75 hostile Yaquis to surrender peacefully even though they threatened to kill him. Some of the group are pictured above.

[SMITHERS COLLECTION, HUMANITIES RESEARCH CENTER
THE UNIVERSITY OF TEXAS AT AUSTIN]

INDEX

Act of February 14, 1903, 9
Act of September 13, 1888, 5
Adams, Mae Palmer, 2
Agua Caliente race track, 124
Agua Prieta, 12, 24, 27, 28
Alamogordo, 53
Albuquerque, 55, 80, 85
Allied Expeditionary Forces, 83
Angel Island Immigration office, 21, 76
Anglos, 52
Arizona, 24, 44
Armistice Day, 92
Avenida Juarez, 35
Avenida Revolución, 120

"banana messenger," 18
bandits, 28
banks, El Paso, 38
Bassett, Bill, 123
Beckett, Officer, 87
Belcher, Jack, 42
Berkshire, F.W., 32, 72
Berlin, Bernie, 123
Birchfield, Charles, 66, 67, 70, 77, 123
Bisbee, 24, 27
Board of Civil Service Examiners, 27
Board of Special Inquiry, 61
border, 58, 65, 73, 105, 120
Border Patrol, viii, ix, 15, 16, 84, 89-91, 93, 95, 100-113, 115, 118, 119
Border Patrol uniform, 91
Border Spanish, 61
Brewster, D.W., 119
Brick, May, 3
Brownsville, 86, 91, 101, 103, 106, 107
Bureau of Immigration and Naturalization, 89
Burnett, Alfred E., 15

Calexico, 123
Calle Comercial, 35
Calumet and Arizona Copper Company, 24
Calzada Jiménez, Fernando, 120, 124, 126
Campbell, Clyde, 103
Canada, 9, 40
Canadian border, 84, 91
Canadian Mounted Police, 90, 91
Carpenter, 60
Carr, Walter E., 91, 100

certificate of residence, 8, 10
Chamizal, 33
Charlie Sam, 50-53
Charlie's killer, 68-70
Chicago, 44
Chihuahua, 25, 26, 37, 48, 79
China, 8, 10, 11, 26, 53
Chinatown, 13, 50-53
Chinese, vii, 5, 6, 8-11, 16, 17, 19-23, 34, 46, 52, 53
Chinese aliens, 13, 44, 45, 49
Chinese Division,
  see outside force, vii, 9, 15, 73, 89, 90
Chinese Exclusion Acts, 5, 8
Chinese hatchmen, 12
Chinese inspectors, 4, 9, 15, 49
Chinese interpreter, 15, 20
Chinese, new, 52
Chinese shopkeepers, 26, 49
Chinese Six Companies, 11-13, 21
"chock chee," 20
Chula Vista, ix
Civil Service, 65, 92
Clark, Frank, 70, 71
Clements, Mannie, 2
comandancia, 39
Congress, 51, 73, 105
contrabandistas, 42
Cordova Island, 42, 86
county jail, 62
"coyote," 68, 74, 79, 80
Crawford Theatre, 1
Customs, Mexican, 67
Customs and Immigrations officers, 46, 55, 84, 111
Customs inspector, 47
Customs Patrol, 83, 84
Customs Service, 9, 47, 87, 110
Customs Service line riders, 9, 84

Dallas, 55, 115-118
Del Rio, 32, 89, 101, 103, 104, 119
Deming, 55
Denver, 85
Department of Labor, 72
Devils River, 89, 91, 119
Díaz, Porfirio, 25
Dickey, Nancy, vii

Douglas, vii, 15, 24-28, 58
Duval County, 110-113

Eagle Pass, 119
Eighteenth Amendment, 83
El General, see Villa, Pancho
El Paso, vii, ix, 1, 3, 26, 32, 34, 36, 39-42, 48, 54, 56, 66, 68, 72-75, 80, 84-87, 89, 91, 94, 95, 103, 107, 110, 123
El Paso Bank and Trust Company, 47
El Paso District, 32, 33, 91, 100
El Paso Milling Company, 74
El Paso police force, 41, 92
El Paso residents, 37
El Paso Sector, 94
El Paso Southwestern night train, 52
Elías, Don Francisco, 26, 28
embargoes against the sale of arms and ammunition to Mexico, 27

Fabens, 103
Falfurrias, 101, 107
fan tan gambling, 51
federal penitentiary, 62
federales, 25, 27, 28, 34, 39, 41, 57
Florida, 91
Forest, 28
Fort Bliss, 1, 59, 93, 95
Fort Lowell, 19
Fort Worth, 55, 115-118

Galveston, 17
gambling in Chinatown, 52
Gardner, Charlie, 66-71
Garner, John Nance, 104, 105
Garrett, Pat, 2
Gay, Portus, 106
Germany, 48, 50
González, Captain, 67
Grand Dragon, 116
Greeks, 79, 80
gringos, 35
Guaymas, 12
gunfights, 86

hacendados, 25, 26
Harne, John, 15, 90, 91
Harris, George J., 32, 90, 100
Heath, Frank, 25, 28
heroin, 47
Home Guard, 72
Hudspeth, Claude, 89, 90

Hueco Street, 63

illegal aliens, 9, 78, 113, 115, 118
illegal entry, 11
Immigrant inspectors,
 see Immigration officers
immigration, 5
Immigration laws and regulations, 61
Immigration officers, 13, 15, 16, 41, 48, 49, 55, 61, 73, 75, 90
Immigration Service, 3, 4, 9, 11, 13, 15, 20, 24, 26, 32-34, 37, 38, 42, 48, 50, 52, 54, 55, 58, 59, 61, 62, 65, 69, 72, 73, 84, 89, 92, 93, 100, 101, 110, 112, 113, 115, 119, 125
Immigration Service detention quarters, 62
Immigration Service Districts, 91
Ings, 49
Inspector-in-Charge, 15
international boundaries, 119
International Bridge, 32, 34, 41, 46, 123

Japanese, 48
Johnson, Lyndon, 33
Jordan, Paul, 77
Juárez, 32-34, 36, 38-42, 45-47, 50, 67, 78-80
Juárez racetrack, 1, 44
Juárez residents, 37

Kansas City, 52, 85
Kansas City railroad yards, 44
Kealy, Jim, 52, 53
Kennedy, John F., 33
Kight, 65, 80, 81, 116
King Ranch, 22
Ku Klux Klan, 116

"La Golondrina," 37
La Junta, 85
La Union, 77
Laredo, 101, 103, 107-110, 112-114, 116, 119
Las Cruces, 80, 82, 103
Las Vegas, 82
line, the, 55, 61
Literacy Act of 1917, 5, 9, 54, 55, 115
Lopez, Red, 27
Los Angeles, 17, 33, 55, 91
Los Angeles District, 91
Luis, 36

Mafia, 79
Manzanillo, 12
Mar Ben, One, 49, 50
Mar Chew, 49
Marfa, 91
Mars, 49
Mayor of Chinatown, 50
Mazatlán, 12
Mexicali, 12
Mexican border, 3, 9, 15, 84, 91
Mexican Immigration Office, 123
Mexican Immigration Service, 125
Mexican railroad section hands, 23
Mexican Revolution, vii, 25, 27, 32, 44, 49
Mexican wetbacks, 106, 118
Mexico, 24, 26, 49, 55
Mexico City, 79
Meyer, 114, 115
Michigan State Police, 90
Military Police, 92
Miller, Walter, 15, 90, 91
Montana Street, 63
Mormons, 25, 26
McKee, Archibald, 53, 72, 73, 84

Nacho's Restaurant, 120
Naco, 12, 15, 27, 28
Nacozari branch line, 29
National Guard, 50
Naval Intelligence, 123
New Orleans, 44
Newman, 52
Nogales, 11, 12, 15, 91
norteamericanos, 40

Office of the United States Commissioner, 62
opium, 52
opium dens in El Paso, 52
Orient, 49
"Orientals," 6
outlaws, 25
outside force, see Chinese Division, 55, 56, 62, 65, 78, 84, 92

Palmer House, 2
Papago Indians, 22
Parr, Archie, 112, 113
Paso del Norte Hotel, 1
Passport Act, 65, 89, 123
Passport officers, 73
Pearson Mills, 70

Pennsylvania Constabulary, 90
Perkins, Clifford Alan, 57, 125
Perkins, Gladys, 58, 63, 64, 72
Perkins, Lyle, 109, 110
Perry, Mrs., 114
Perry, Willis B., 62, 92, 95, 96, 113, 114
Pershing, John J., 51
Phelps-Dodge Copper Company, 24
Phoenix, 10, 22, 55
pimps, 115, 117
Pirtleville, 24
plainclothesman, 18
polygamy, 25
Port Isabel, 86
Powers, Pat, 2
Powers, Tom, 2
Prohibition, 55, 96, 97, 115
Prohibition Enforcement Act, 83
Prohibition officers, 84, 87, 96
prostitutes, 46, 52, 112-117

Quota Law of 1921, 5, 79

racetrack followers, 45
Railroad Avenue, 81
Railway Mail Service, 92
Raton, 79, 81
Rawls Fletcher, 65, 103, 116
red-light district, 4
refugees, 37
"Reminiscences of a Chinese inspector," viii
Republican Party, 106
revolutionaries, 28
Rio Grande, 1, 27, 56, 65, 66, 79, 83, 89, 100, 102, 111
Rio Grande City, 86, 106, 107, 119
Rio Grande Valley, 86, 104, 106
Roberts, Kenneth L., 118, 119
Rodríguez, 40-42
rurales, 28, 67

St. Louis, 80
San Antonio, 33, 93, 103, 112, 113, 116-119
San Antonio District, 91, 100, 101, 108, 115
San Antonio Division, viii
San Diego, 110-112
San Francisco, 12
San Francisco earthquake and fire, 13
San Luis Obispo, 91

San Ysidro, viii, 120, 123
Sánchez Aldana, Moisés, 123
Santa Fe, 82
Santa Fe Railroad, 54
Santa Fe Street Bridge, 33, 60
Santa Rita Hotel, 5
Saturday Evening Post, 119
Secretary of Commerce and Labor, 9
Service, the, *see* Immigration Service
Seventh Cavalry, 92
Shangai, 12
Shanghai Low Restaurant, 20
Sherman Hog Ranch, 87, 88
Sierra, Antonio, 25
Sierra Blanca, 91
smelter district, 1, 57, 58, 66
smugglers, 21, 42, 44, 45, 56-58, 60-63, 74, 75, 82, 95, 86, 96, 97, 103, 111, 113, 114
smuggling, 54, 55, 67, 110, 118
smuggling of guns and ammunition, 40
smuggling of opium, 12, 50
Socorro, 82
Sonnichsen, C.L., viii
Sonora, 25, 26
Southern Pacific passenger and freight trains, 15, 54, 55
spotters, 60, 61
Stanton Street Bridge, 33, 70, 74
Stevens, Charles, 58, 59
Strauss, New Mexico, 77, 78
sweat boxes, 45

Taylor, Don, 120
Texas, 44
Texas Rangers, 101, 102, 113
Tijuana, 123, 124
Tijuana Valley, 123

Tisdale, 95, 116
Torreón, 48
Torres, Pete, 65, 96
Treasury Department, 84
Truesdale, 65
Tucson, vii, 4, 10, 11, 15, 16, 18, 21, 25, 91
Tucson inspectors, 20

Union Depot, 56, 57
United States Army, 34, 65, 93, 95, 102
United States Army Cavalry, 27
United States collector of internal revenue, 10
United States Commissioner, 5
Utah, 25

Valladolid, Rodolfo, 120
Villa, Luz Corral de, 40, 41
Villa, Pancho, vii, 33-40, 42-44, 51
Villa money, 38
Villistas, 33, 35, 37-39, 43

Waco, 118
War Act, 83
Washington D.C., 84
West Coast, 24
Whalen, 103-105
white slave trade, 12
Wilson government, 27, 41
Wilson, Woodrow, 40, 83
Woods, Officer, 87
Wongs, 49
World War I, 49, 65, 71, 73
World War II, 123

Yaqui Indians, 27
Yuma, 18, 32, 91

Zapata, Emiliano, 25

Two Border Patrolmen watching a crossing on the Rio Grande near Presidio, Texas where smugglers delivered bootlegged liquor in 1928.
[SMITHERS COLLECTION, HUMANITIES RESEARCH CENTER
THE UNIVERSITY OF TEXAS AT AUSTIN]

Seven Border Patrolmen in 1928 near Presidio, Texas: Earl Hill, Fred Reader, Emmett Hunter, Chief Ivan Williams, E. C. Dennis, John R. Cain, and Edwin Dorn, all veterans of World War I.
[SMITHERS COLLECTION, HUMANITIES RESEARCH CENTER
THE UNIVERSITY OF TEXAS AT AUSTIN]